THE ROAD TO ANYWHERE

By the same author:

Lucretius, Prophet of the Atom
Richard N. Skinner
(Fulmen, 2003)

A THE ROAD TO NYWHERE

Reflections on cruising under sail

DICK SKINNER

FULMEN PUBLICATIONS
2005

First published in England in 2005
by Fulmen Publications
4 St. Michael's Court
Manningtree
Essex CO11 1BH

A CIP catalogue record for this book is available
from the British Library

ISBN 0 9545334 1 0

Produced by Pagewise
2 Butlers Close
Amersham
Bucks HP6 5PY

Art direction, design and coordination
Mónica Bratt
monicabratt@onetel.com

Printed and bound in England
by Biddles Ltd

Contents

Acknowledgements and Apologies

Some of the stories recounted here first appeared in articles published by *Yachting World* and *Yachting Monthly*, as did several of the photographs. My thanks are due to the editors of those journals for the encouragement they gave me to write about sailing.

I am also grateful to Peter Jenkins for letting me use pictures taken some years ago by his father Ford Jenkins, and to Pär Bäckström of Norrländska Socialdemokraten [NSD] in Luleå for permission to use the photographs he took on one of our visits there.

For this book to work it has to stay focused on the multi-layered experience of cruising under sail. Some details have had to be given of events ashore which influenced life afloat, but much of great personal significance has had to be omitted.

This means that the debt owed to those who sailed with me in earlier years,and gave me the benefit of their greater knowledge of the ways of the sea, remains unpaid. Perhaps it never could be. Then I recall the help provided by members of the Little Ship Club and the Cruising Association, both at home and overseas. All my voyages were under the burgee of one or the other. Fellow Vega and Vancouver skippers have also been a source of information and companionship over many years.

Much could equally have been said of friends in Germany, Poland, Sweden and Finland who offered the hospitality and local knowledge that made our travels so worthwhile. A brief mention has been made of some, all too brief, because to list them all would have turned this book into into one long catalogue of thanks.

The independence we seek at sea is real enough, and achievable. Yet what makes it possible is the help we receive from others. It is hoped that all readers will be as fortunate in this respect as I have been.

CHAPTER ONE

Of Rivers and Reedbeds

I T ALL BEGAN WITH WATER AND REEDBEDS; water which moved sluggishly under the influence of a distant sea, and reeds that softened the banks of the winding rivers of Broadland. Or perhaps it rose with the streaks of mist that gathered over the marshes on a fine evening to form a soft white carpet from which the willows projected to mark the course of the river. Yet the very mention of mist makes me think it started with a dream inherited from my father. At any rate it began quite early in life, when my sister and I were still at school.

In those days the family would take short, war-time holidays in Beccles, perched above the Waveney valley on what is said to have been once a cliff bordering the sea. These breaks became precious to us all, and Beccles came to hold a special place in our affections. At the weekend a Salvation Army band would play in the square, while the Italian prisoners of war, who worked on farms nearby, would gather to listen to the music and join the locals in a gentle *passeggiata*. We stayed in a hotel looking on to the square which possessed an elderly night porter who would regale guests with his account of the bomb which had fallen on the Surrey Street bus station in Norwich, the day that war came to East Anglia. We all listened politely each time the tale was told, but somehow failed to take it to heart. We lived in London and had been bombed, off and on, for some years.

In the evening my father would lead us out to watch the mist rising and promise us a sunny day to follow. Meteorologically the phenomenon may have said more about the day that had passed than about the one to come, but who were we to quibble? Besides he was always right. It never rained in those days, or so it now seems.

That ritual gaze over the river valley was for my father a look back in time. He carried with him a rather patchy memory of sailing on the Broads as a young man, when the world was at peace and yachts without engines were the norm, to be propelled by long quant poles should the wind fail. Chance had opened a door for him, which had closed again before he had mastered the art of sailing, leaving an unrequited dream that drifted with the mist over the marshes and the river Waveney.

So it was not exactly chance that took us down the hill to hire a boat and venture on to the water. A flat-bottomed boat with a small and erratic outboard motor may seem an unlikely first step towards the realisation of an ideal, but it was all that was available to us at the time. We borrowed some fishing tackle to go with it, bought a tin of maggots, and set out.

It was soon apparent that oars were more reliable than the little motor, and much more fun. On most days I would row our unwieldy craft upstream towards Geldeston Lock, stopping on the way to picnic or to engage in a battle of wits with the roach, bream or perch that inhabited these waters. It was a battle that the fish usually won, treating us with the contempt they reserve for rank beginners.

It is easy, after years at sea, attempting to master the problems of navigation or of handling small yachts in nasty weather to forget the simple pleasures of rowing. To pass under the bridges at Beccles and hear the click of the oars in their rowlocks change to a more hollow sound invokes a feeling of childish delight, while to glide noiselessly beside the reedbeds and discover the meticulously woven nest of a reed warbler is magic at any age. Even a struggle against tide or headwind can produce over your whole body from the soles of your feet to the tips of your fingers feelings of direct, physical satisfaction that no motor could ever match.

Yet it was to a motor boat that my father turned, when the war was over. I suspect that he did not feel confident of his own, or his family's, ability to sail a Broads yacht, or perhaps he had reached an age where he felt a little more comfort was required. If his choice of craft lacked boldness, his timing was nevertheless a token of his dedication to a youthful dream. For he had by then left government service and rejoined his pre-war firm, and while his friends and colleagues were rushing to re-equip with cars now that petrol was once again available, he bought a boat.

In this he had the enthusiastic support of his family. My mother became the most assiduous of boatwives, while my sister and I assumed from the start that we were full members of the ship's complement. It appeared to us to be entirely natural to prefer a boat to a car, even if the logistics involved were at times somewhat onerous. We became accustomed to the walk to the station, laden with heavy bags, to changing trains, once in London and again at Norwich, and to carrying our luggage from the station at Brundall to the boatyard where our acquisition lay. But to speak of a boat as an acquisition would have seemed strange to us even then. You do not own a boat, any more than you own a wife or a dog. It would be truer to say the boat owns you.

She was an old boat, designed for use on the Upper Thames, and quite unlike most Broads motor cruisers. Her cockpit was sheltered by a fixed, wooden canopy, carried on four steel posts. From this canvas curtains could be let down to turn the cockpit into a sleeping room at night. She leaked, from below and from above so that it was impossible to guarantee anyone a dry night's sleep. Her gear box was chancy and the engine of a type long obsolete. It was obvious that a great deal of work needed to be done.

Most of this was left to the boat yard, but some we did ourselves. Of course we lacked experience, but had at least some time available to help put things in order. My sister had not yet left home to work in a children's nursery, while I was waiting to go to university after completing my army service in the Middle East. The boat was given a new engine, her seams were caulked and her decks re-covered to keep out the rain. My mother and sister went over every inch of her inside, cleaning out the dust of ages and chasing away the resident spiders.

My main contribution was the purchase of a dinghy, a brand-new, clinker-built twelve footer that rowed well but could be rigged as a sailing boat with a single lugsail. Most of the money to buy it came from savings made during my service overseas. Army pay had hardly been excessive, but opportunities for spending money had proved sparse during some months in hospital in the desert. So I had built myself a small gratuity that was used to further an ambition which at the time I perceived only vaguely.

Well, there I was with my first sailing boat. Her varnished mahogany planking gleamed and her tanned gaff sail, small as it was, was entirely in keeping with the tradition of the Broads. Now all that was needed was to learn to sail. It would not be correct to say that I had had no formal training. Before I fell ill in Egypt I had had one lesson. This was at a sailing club for service personnel on the Great Bitter Lake. There were highly competent German instructors at the club. If this seems strange, given that the war in Europe had finished some years before, the answer lies in politics. There were indeed a number of Germans running leisure facilities for the troops. I used to visit one of the canteens they manned in our camp to play table tennis with them. They were of course older men, patiently awaiting a belated repatriation. Their problem was that they came from what was by then the Russian zone in Germany and for their own safety were looking to be resettled elsewhere.

My sailing instructor was pleasant enough. That we did not exactly see eye to eye had nothing to do with nationality, but rested on my natural aversion to instruction of any kind, and especially of the military kind. A series of sharp commands threw me into a state of abject confusion, while his reaction to my admission that I could not swim set the seal on our lack of mutual understanding. How could I presume to sail if I could not swim? Perhaps I might have reminded him that the British navy had been made great by whole crews of non-swimmers, but I was by then in no state to argue.

His last command as he sent me ashore was to fold the sail and put it away. There was a wind blowing at the time and as soon as I had one end folded and held down, the other unravelled in the breeze. At length an attractive girl in army uniform, observing my predicament, came down from the clubhouse to lend a hand. Later I was to see this as an opportunity lost. At the time it served to complete my humiliation and I scurried away, never to return.

So it was that when once I had a boat of my own, I bought a book on sailing and set out to see if it all worked. Later I was lucky enough to find a middle path between military discipline and trial-and-error, but in the case of a small, lugsail dinghy there is much in favour of trial-and-error. This is especially so on Broadland rivers. They develop that sixth sense a sailor has to have, a feeling for the wind and what it is likely to do next.

There are trees which, even singly and at a distance, may rob you of your motive power. Then you come to learn the patience needed to drift through the dead patches and the quick reactions required when the wind hits you again, probably from a different direction. And while you are learning you are seldom alone. Even in those days it was necessary to keep an eye open for other craft. In particular there were motor boats of all shapes and sizes, some driven by people of little experience, or even by their children. Which introduced you to the great, unwritten law of navigation: 'small gives way to large'.

With the dinghy in tow our family embarked on a thorough exploration of Broadland. The Broads themselves are quite small, shallow lakes. They are linked by rivers, the Bure with its tributaries in the northern part and the rivers Yare and Waveney to the south. These rivers unite at Yarmouth to flow out to sea under the Haven Bridge. Here the tide runs fast and great care has to be taken in the narrow channel that goes through the town. Hirers of boats are given awful warnings of the dangers of taking a wrong turn and passing under the Haven Bridge into that part of the river reserved for seagoing craft.

Thus it is easy to see the Broads as two distinct areas, north and south, but even within these areas there are pronounced differences in character between the calm, tree-lined upper reaches and the wilder, estuarial stretches that succeed them. It is only the reed beds extending almost all the way to Yarmouth which provide continuity. So although Broadland is a fairly compact region it does not lack variety – enough, for those who love it, to last a lifetime.

We took our boat wherever the bridges were not so low as to prevent our quaint canopy from passing under. Even then we were able to explore further in the dinghy. A row of three or four miles was welcome exercise. We became familiar with coots, grebes, kingfishers and the tall grey herons that stood sentry on almost every reach. Herons flying low over the marshes or standing perfectly still waiting for unwary fish seemed at first to be solitary birds. We imagined them building isolated nests among the reeds, rather like swans. That is, until the evening when we rowed past the woods beyond Surlingham and saw what a heronry was really like – nests high in the trees and dozens of the great birds wheeling in all directions, wooing or threatening each other with their harsh cries.

Then there were times when we found a sheltered place and tied our dinghy to a clump of reeds to fish for an hour or two, and times when we moored alongside a Broadland pub to sample the beers that were available, Steward and Pattesons, Lacons, Morgans, Bullards, names long gone.

Our greatest adventure was a voyage on Breydon Water, an open stretch of estuary almost four miles long. Here you were exposed to the full force of the wind, and even to something like waves. A channel marked by wooden posts ran through the mud flats on either side, and on these posts sat cormorants, stretching out their wings to dry, and black-backed gulls with bright yellow beaks, real sea birds.

I see us returning from excursions of this kind, motoring steadily up river in the afternoon sunshine when the shadows were lengthening, with an image of our strange craft with its high canopy projected on to the tall reeds to starboard, accompanying us on the last miles home.

It would be easy to believe that we belonged there, in this water-based world with its reeds and its birds, but the hard fact is that most of our time was spent on dry land. Events ashore mattered to us then, and ultimately were to cast their own shadows on the water.

My father progressed rapidly in his post-war career, and was soon able to buy the car he had so bravely forfeited in favour of a boat. There was now money enough for both. He was however exceedingly busy, so for him leisure time became both scarce and precious. My mother also was fully occupied looking after first one and then the other of her parents in their declining years. My sister had taken a job in a children's home, and so was away for much of the time. I had gone to my university hoping to find in a study of Classics some fundamental truths, only to find myself in something of a minority. What is more, for the first time in my life I was in the company of young women, and learning the most elementary facts about them was a process that carried at least as much pain as pleasure. But during this time of delayed adolescence I, of all the family, had some leisure time to spare, at least in summer.

Initially this caused some tension between us, since I naturally wanted to borrow the boat to take mixed parties of friends on the water. My father acquiesced reluctantly, clearly embarrassed at the thought of what might – and indeed did – happen. In return for his forbearance, I was available to accompany him on those occasions when he could get away from his work. So in those days the ship's complement was often just the two of us.

We would cruise mainly on the southern rivers, seeking out the best bakers and butchers, cooking our own meals and spending evenings in favourite pubs or at isolated moorings we had discovered in the course of our travels. We used the dinghy a great deal, mainly in its role as a rowing boat. Sailing was better done single-handed, once I had seen my father's difficulty in moving about the cluttered and volatile craft it became under sail. Two memories of that time persist. The sequence of events has long been lost, but does not matter. In one scene we are rowing quietly in the last of the evening light along a tree-lined reach of the river Waveney. I had rested the oars to create a silence in which we could look around for any wildlife that might be active. In this mode we glided under a willow and looked up at a branch almost immediately above our heads. On it were three magpies snuggled close together, side by side, and fast asleep. Had we wished we could have reached up and tickled their breast feathers. As it was we held our breath and let the boat drift on, out beyond the shade of the willow, to row quietly back to our own bunks.

The second picture is at the other end of the Broadland spectrum. It is again evening, but we are moored outside a busy pub, with as many boats as could find room at the quay. When we had eaten and washed up we went into the bar for a pint or two. In the far corner of the room was a piano in full cry, while the crowded bar was buzzing with chat. We were into our second pint when the door opened and three young men came in, one of whom was playing a clarinet. He played so well that gradually the talk subsided, the piano fell silent and everyone sat, sipping ale and listening. The word spellbound might be appropriate here, because when closing time came the young men left with the clarinettist still playing and everyone followed him out on to the quayside, as if he were the Pied Piper. For a few minutes more he played on, while a cheerful crowd stood around him on the lawn in front of the pub, and we sat on the cabin top of our boat, under the starlight, listening.

Many years later I visited the area by car and saw that pub again. It was a grey day in winter, with a cold wind blowing. Somehow the whole place seemed smaller than I remembered it. Could the bar really have held all those people and a piano? The lawn outside now appeared as a patch of unkempt grass over which scraps of paper and the odd plastic bag were rustling in the chilly breeze.

Memories are of course selective, and not only those we choose consciously to pass on. Mostly the selection is automatic, tuning out those, for example, that are embarrassing to us, so that they either disappear altogether or are relegated to a sealed store, to be opened only when a corrective to pride is required. Others stand outside this convenient and comforting process. They are fixed and hard, ready to surface at any time, and quite immune to conscious or unconscious control.

The next years produced two of this sort, one totally distressing and the other entirely beneficial, which had a huge impact on all our lives, and ultimately on that part of my life which was spent afloat. I had by then left college and embarked, albeit reluctantly, on a career in business. My mother had seen both her parents to their graves and was beginning to recover, very slowly, from the stress of caring for them. Then my sister fell ill and quite suddenly died.

Just as veterans of warfare may carry in their bodies fragments of shrapnel that cannot be removed, so my parents and I had from then the shock and grief of that event embedded firmly in our minds. It stayed with them for the rest of their lives and will stay with me for the rest of mine.

Naturally it drew us closer together, as I assumed the responsibilities of an only child. Yet other influences were pulling in the opposite direction. For one thing, the boat had to go. Whether this was a natural evolution or reflected a need to escape painful reminders of happier times, I cannot say. My parents decided to buy a smaller motor boat, brand new and very handsome, but with room, in practical terms, for just the two of them. At the same time I wanted to do some real sailing in a boat of my own, and, with some financial help from my mother, settled on a two-berth Broads yacht, which was in fact a retired hire-craft. So it is clear that some centrifugal forces were at work.

The force that was driving me was the oldest known to man. I had thoughts of getting married. Joy and I had met at college some years before and had shared a love of talk, of poetry and of the best food we could at that time afford. We had remained friends ever since, until it eventually became clear to both of us that no one else was likely to be quite so tolerant of our various eccentricities. There is always some danger in changing a relationship from friendship to something else, but in our case the risk was minimal: 'friendship' just became 'friendship plus'.

It was obvious that our marriage would affect life afloat, but I could not have predicted the extent and direction of the changes that would eventually follow. As far as I was concerned the great idea was to share the experience of sailing my dearly-loved Broadland rivers. I knew that Joy was happy to join me in this. What I did not appreciate was her capacity for developing much wider and wilder ideas of what sailing was all about. However, for the time being ignorance was sheer bliss.

The boat we had was called 'Wild Rose'. She was about twenty one feet long and had a true Broads gaff rig, with a mast that could be lowered to get her under bridges. The tiny cabin had two berths, while cooking was done in the cockpit, the stove sharing the space with a little one and a half horsepower two-stroke engine.

Broads yachts normally have the mast stepped quite far forward, so that they carry a small foresail and a much larger mainsail, on a boom which often extends out beyond the stern. The advantage of this gaff sail is that a large proportion of the sail area is carried high, enabling it to catch as much as possible of the wind blowing over the tall reedbeds. The gaff also has a steadying effect, so that momentum can be maintained through dead patches caused by trees or buildings. The net result on warm but breezy days is that you can sit, basking in the sunlight, sheltered from the wind by the reeds, while your boat tears along at a fine pace – an experience so delightful that I could not then imagine sailing without those heaven-sent reedbeds.

The reedbeds also offered opportunities for relaxation. There were occasions when we would round up into the wind, nose into the bank and tie the bow to a handful of reeds. The stern was left to swing freely, the gaff lowered half-way and the boom raised, so that the sail lost all power and the boat lay quietly head to wind. In this mode passing craft caused little disturbance. The stern would rise gently in their wake and subside again with no splashing or bumping.

There were a number of favourite spots for this. One that appealed to our sense of irony was in the lee of some trees upstream from the Cantley sugar beet factory. Cantley itself was out of sight, so that we might have been miles away from anything industrial or ugly, and the only sound to be heard came from the wood pigeons in the trees around Langley.

Perhaps the best of that first year together came in October, when the season was nearly over. Then we made an expedition down towards Breydon Water, when every evening saw the mists gathering and waterside pubs were lighting wood fires in their grates. At the end of the day the water was almost still, apart from the V-shaped wakes of coypu swimming across the river. These large beasts had almost replaced the water voles of my childhood. They were however similar in many ways. They were rodents, about a metre long, with large front teeth and an entirely peaceful disposition.

The coypu is a native of South America that had been imported to be bred for its fur, called nutria by the furriers. A number had escaped and had found the Broads very much to their liking. They loved water and would happily make their homes in the banks of rivers. Most types of greenstuff would serve as food, including crops growing in the nearby fields.

This was to prove their downfall. To be accused of undermining river banks is one thing: it seems doubtful if anyone cared much about that, or could really distinguish the damage their burrows caused from that made by the wash of motor vessels. But to eat the farmers' crops, or even to be suspected of it, merited a death sentence – and the farmers had guns. Since coypu were not a native species the slaughter of what were known locally as 'nooter rats' received official encouragement. These beautiful creatures became extinct and their cries were no longer heard over the marshes at night.

Within a couple of years we had company on our voyages

around the Broads. Fortunately our daughter Katy was a small child who could be fitted somehow into the cabin with us and as she grew older we obtained a chair that could be set up over the cockpit coaming at meal times, and a strong line to ensure that she remained attached to the boat.

This sort of boating was one way in which a father who worked long hours and was quite frequently away from home could get to know his child. Children on boats are never neglected: they are perforce under the eye of their parents twenty four hours a day. Clearly they relish the attention given them, but there is an advantage for fathers as well, beyond the obvious one of getting to know their children better. This is the discipline that is instilled automatically by the very nature of life afloat. For whatever needs children may have, or think they have, they soon learn that the needs of the boat come first. That of course did not prevent one father from jumping into a dinghy to rescue a Teddy bear that had been cast carelessly overboard and was fast drifting away on the tide, but at a later stage it did make the dual role of father and skipper a little easier.

By this time our life in Broadland had become better organised. My father had bought a riverside plot at Brundall, where both our boats could be moored. We would sometimes cruise in company and occasionally swap crews, so that my father did in the end sail a Broads yacht once more. But for the most part Joy and Katy and I continued our explorations in 'Wild Rose', swinging our mast between the trees of the upper reaches, sliding sideways into small spaces left on crowded quays, and learning what we could about handling boats under sail alone.

Life afloat might have continued in this way indefinitely had it not been for the attraction the sea held for Joy. Had not her brothers trained for the merchant service? Real sailors, as far as she was concerned, went to sea. Now the sea was not all that far away and could be reached from the Broads at two points. One, as we have seen, was Yarmouth Haven; the other was Lowestoft Harbour, which was connected to Oulton Broad by Mutford Lock and the not inappropriately named Lake Lothing. As it happened the owner of our local boatyard made a pilgrimage to sea each year, going out at Lowestoft and returning through Yarmouth. Why could we not do something similar?

So quite early one morning I found myself lowering the mast and motoring through Mutford Lock and under a couple of bridges into Lowestoft harbour. There the mast was raised again, not without some difficulty in the swell that came in from the sea outside. Then we headed for the harbour entrance and, as the piers opened out, I saw a sea lit by the easterly sun with a silvery light that illuminated every wave, right to the horizon, and indeed beyond. In that moment I realised that this was the road to everywhere. The sea would take me anywhere I wished, provided only that I had the time and the skill to accept what it offered.

Just then the feeling was momentary, since once we were clear of the land what had seemed a sizeable yacht shrank to something quite insignificant, and extremely vulnerable. Dipping and rolling in the unfamiliar movement of the waves, we concentrated all our effort into getting safely into Yarmouth and back to our reed-bound waters. For that year we were content with our one great adventure.

For sailors winter is a time for dreaming dreams and making plans. Last year's cruise has been recorded in the log book, whether a source of satisfaction or frustration – or more likely of both – it is finished and done with. What matters is where to go next. Now for us there was nowhere new to go in the Broads: any cruise we might plan would be a variation on the theme of cruises past. There was nothing wrong with that, of course, but the spirit of adventure, once invoked, is hard to put back in its bottle. Joy had tasted a couple of hours of life at sea and wanted more, while I was finding that my short moment of revelation in Lowestoft Harbour had come to occupy a permanent place in my mind. So another sea trip was planned.

This time we would ride the spring north easterlies south to Aldeburgh. The distance was such that the sea voyage, before entering the river that led back north to Aldeburgh, could be accomplished with the flood stream to speed us on. The way in from the sea at Shingle Street is a narrow channel between sand-banks which is liable to change direction every year after the gales of winter. It is best attempted well into a rising tide. In retrospect it does not seem an entrance that should have attracted beginners, but the alternatives on that part of the coast north of Harwich are just as tricky, and we had the confidence of ignorance.

Which is why, one evening in May, 'Wild Rose' crept into Lowestoft Harbour to await the morning tide. We had made some preparations for the task ahead of us. An anchor had been bought and provision made for navigation lights. We had a cot for Katy, which could be wedged safely on one of our bunks when at sea, and a child's push chair, folded down and lashed behind the mast.

The morning forecast was as good as could be expected: a north easterly wind of moderate strength (force 3 or 4). The local boat-man assured us that with wind and tide together the sea would be 'like a mill pond'. Now, if ever, was the time to go.

The mill pond turned out to be quite boisterous with sizeable waves and numerous 'white horses'. Fortunately the direction of the wind remained constant, but its strength was clearly greater than had been forecast. Movement on the boat made tasks such as nappy-changing hazardous and words quite unlike those of motherly love floated up to me from the cabin. When Joy emerged, somewhat ruffled, it was to face our first emergency at sea.

The shrouds which held our mast in position were tensioned with bottle-screws. One of these had come undone as a result of the movement on the boat. Naturally it was not under tension at the time, so there was no immediate danger all the while the mast was supported from the other side, but should we have to change tack the consequences did not bear contemplation. So while I held the boat as steady as possible Joy went forward with a length of twine to lash the shroud back in place. In a boat with no guard rail and without any safety-harness – harnesses were not in general use at that time – this called for a good sense of balance. It was the pre-cursor of many trips she made in boats that needed a sail change or an extra lashing put in place, but never again did she have to tie down a shroud. We quickly learned to lock bottle screws in position for work at sea.

With a favourable wind 'Wild Rose' shot through the entrance to the river in grand style. Inside progress was slow as we turned north and motored against the wind up to Aldeburgh. We were cold and tired by the time we arrived at Slaughden Quay to pick up a vacant mooring.

The mooring we had chanced on was marked by a substantial buoy with a loop of heavy rope on top. We passed a rope of our own through this and made fast, only to see a boat rowing purposefully towards us, propelled by a tough-looking seaman in a jersey and wearing earrings. 'No, no sir, that may be all right on your Broads, sir, but it's chains here, sir, chains!' So I had to haul the buoy aboard and make fast with the chain suspended from it. This was our introduction to Jumbo Ward, who looked after boats, buoys and Broads sailors with commendable care and patience.

There is nothing soft about Aldeburgh. Its beach is shingly and bleak, exposed to the full force of easterly gales. In the town there are submerged tensions between townsfolk born and bred, the arty-crafty community which has grown up around the musical enterprise of Benjamin Britten, and summer visitors, including visiting yachtsmen. Peter Grimes lives on and Britten's music truly represents the nature of his town.

The road from the town to the yacht club at Slaughden Quay runs along a windswept sandbank that separates sea from river. It was on this road that Katy learned to walk, or almost to sail as the push chair to which she was clinging was bowled along in the breeze from the sea. But by then we were getting used to anxious moments.

In the club we were treated most kindly, with no hint of disapproval of our rashness in leaving the safety of the Broads for a more testing environment. Those were times when it was still accepted that learning meant stretching one's abilities beyond what was entirely prudent. Besides, no one went to sea from Aldeburgh without some element of risk.

On our way south again we anchored for a night off Havergate Island. This is a sanctuary for sea birds of several kinds, including avocets with their graceful curved bills. The whole area was then – and is now for the most part – bleak and wild, populated by creatures quite unlike the coypu and kingfishers with which we were familiar. At the river entrance between the sandbanks it was sometimes possible to meet a seal. The distance from there to the heart of Broadland was not great, yet it seemed that we were dealing with two different worlds. It did not occur to me then that we would have to choose which of them to inhabit.

Light southerly winds brought us home to Lowestoft and through to Oulton Broad. There we stopped for a while so that a professional photographer could take pictures of 'Wild Rose'. It is hard to recall the precise motive for this. It may have been pride in a boat which had broken free of the Broads and completed a successful voyage south, but I suspect that there was something valedictory about it. Katy was growing fast and for that reason, if for no other, we would shortly have to say goodbye to our first and much-loved boat. Pride had its place however. Looking at the pictures taken I notice that the push chair had been removed from the deck before photography. It was by then a sorry object that had gone completely rusty in the salt spray from the North Sea.

CHAPTER TWO

A Passion for Navigation

C HOOSING A NEW BOAT WAS NOT EASY, given our limited financial resources. 'Wild Rose' had been a one-off design, hand-built with mahogany planking. We had now to select from a limited range of production models. The boat we chose was called an Audacity. She was the same length as 'Wild Rose' but made of moulded plywood. There were four berths, a more powerful engine and the cooking could be done in the cabin. In fact, although there was room for no more than a single burner cooker, this could be fully gimballed so that it was remarkably steady at sea, and whoever happened to be the cook could work sitting on the centre-board case, which ran the length of the cabin.

The idea of a centre-board was to provide a deeper keel and hence greater stability when the board was lowered. When raised it enabled the boat to stay afloat in about half a metre of water. It appeared to us to be an ideal feature for a boat which was to divide its time between the open sea and the shallow Broads. There were however disadvantages, of which we were at the time only vaguely aware. Centre-boards are of limited efficiency and can be an embarrassment should they become jammed when fully down. The casing, apart from providing a perch for the cook, was a thorough nuisance in the cabin, and the lowering mechanism was a steel wire that ran through a hole in the top of it. Looking at this ashore as a prospective buyer does nothing to prepare you for the jet of water which comes up through that hole in a lumpy sea; a little, watery tree with fern-like branches.

The Audacity was of course a compromise, but it was one which reflected well our own compromised stance, looking both inland and out to sea. For the next three seasons we remained based on our riverside mooring, with annual excursions out through Mutford Lock or Yarmouth Haven as far as Pin Mill on the River Orwell and the Walton Backwaters. As our voyages lengthened the risks attached to them increased. We had a great deal to learn, and while the 'trial and error' method had worked well on the Broads, commuting between Harwich Harbour and Lowestoft once a year did not provide enough practice to tackle the North Sea.

Aware of this I enrolled for a series of navigation classes at the Little Ship Club in London. These were excellent and certainly increased my desire to understand more of the black arts involved. But lectures, however good, can only warn and advise. They cannot of their own accord instil in you the judgement required to know when to turn back rather than carry on, nor equip you adequately for what may happen if you sail into the night unprepared either physically or mentally. Lessons of this kind have to be learned the hard way: in our case by stranding our boat on Pakefield beach in pitch darkness, totally confused by the light of street lamps strung along the shore.

It is possible now to say that this was the only serious accident we had in over forty years. Naturally enough we made mistakes throughout all the time we spent sailing together, but were usually able to get ourselves out of trouble. Either we would see more options open to us, which is the product of experience, or we were simply luckier on other occasions. Mostly we tended to avoid situations that were potentially dangerous, even if that meant waiting in harbour.

But on that night all of this was in the future. Looking at our boat stranded on the beach we reacted as I suspect most couples would. That is to say, I was consumed by shame at my failure as a skipper, while Joy went quietly about salvaging everything possible from the disaster. Perhaps I am wrong in supposing that all women display a more practical turn of mind in such circumstances. Some might be put off boating for life – mine was not.

The boat was towed off the beach the next day, and repaired over the following winter. Our own recovery took longer. This was due to a combination of events, the most significant of which had nothing to do with sailing. It was a period of domestic turmoil. I had a new job which entailed moving house nearer to the centre of England, while Joy was busy rearing our second daughter, Helen. Time for boating was scarce while, if we had been able to manage one child aboard without too much trouble, the combination of a baby and an active five-year-old was formidable. We retreated to the Broads for a couple of years until we were able to face up to the choice that had to be made.

This choice did not include the possibility of giving up sailing. Although my confidence had been dented neither of us ever suggested that or, as far as I know, ever thought of it. In token of our determination to carry on we had a house built on a plot of land some miles to the east of my office, to shorten the journey to the coast. The question was not whether to sail, but rather where to sail. We could no longer pretend to be both Broads sailors and sea sailors: it had to be one or the other.

So we left the comfort of the riverside plot at Brundall and took a swinging mooring on the River Orwell at Woolverstone. From there we could slip downstream to Harwich Harbour and, in course of time, explore all the East Coast rivers from the Alde to the Medway. To do this we had to find our way between sandbanks and through swatchways, always mindful of the depth of water under our keel.

As a training ground in the art of pilotage the Thames Estuary was supreme. At high tide there were no dangers to be seen; they were all under water. In poor visibility you groped your way from one buoy to the next. When the weather was clear you might see buoys all around, but which was the one you wanted? The wrong choice could take you straight on to a sandbank. Nowadays yachtsmen use satellite navigation equipment to tell them where they are, and press a button to learn what course the machine tells them to steer next. It was more fun to go armed only with a chart, a compass and a depth sounder.

Although the children had by then adjusted well to life afloat, and were completely unperturbed by the motion of the boat at sea, they did demand frequent trips ashore, especially to beaches where they could play. Joy bore the brunt of this, ferrying them to and fro in the dinghy. I had no great liking for the sand and mud such expeditions attracted, but made an exception in the case of what Katy had designated 'tree horses'.

These were a feature of the foreshore opposite our mooring on the Orwell. Trees undermined by water had blown down so that they rested on their strongest boughs, with their trunks horizontal. These became horses which the children could ride into whatever fantasy they chose. I think I rather envied them their steeds, feeling the extent to which my own imagination had become circumscribed. Perhaps it is clearer to me now that my tree horse was the boat itself, and subsequent boats even more so.

Katy had by then learned to row, and could be left to work her way across the tidal stream and return safely to the yacht. Helen's first successful attempt was in Yokesfleet Creek, off the River Roach. We dropped anchor here one evening and as the tide ebbed, found ourselves surrounded by huge banks of mud that took on a range of delicate hues as the water retreated into a narrow channel. We were quite alone and nothing of the world was to be seen above the mudbanks. Katy played her flute, while Helen took command of the dinghy, under the watchful eye of her mother, and when we eventually retired to our bunks we were lulled to sleep by the rumble of the engines of great ships making their way up the Thames, just the other side of the marshes that encompassed our safe anchorage.

It is not surprising that the memories which come most frequently to mind from those days are centred on our own River Orwell. The Orwell is navigable from Harwich Harbour right up to Ipswich, and even then was used by quite large vessels. Such ships were a hazard to small boat sailors but did not detract from the beauty of the river itself with its wooded banks and a wonderful bay at Pin Mill which possessed then, and still does today, one of the finest pubs in England, a place where the high tide could come right up to the window of the bar, and recede to reveal a great stretch of mud dotted with boats drying out, a place where sea boots were quite acceptable, even if they did leave a few puddles on the stone floor. The ships that could be seen passing Potter Point merely served to emphasise the continuity between this sheltered spot and the sea outside.

On a weekend visit we would sail early in the morning when the river was quiet. In springtime our departure was marked by the sound of a cuckoo calling in the woods at Woolverstone; then, when we had reached Pin Mill and were approaching the next stand of trees, a rival bird would be heard, shouting in competition. So that we seemed to be passed from one cuckoo to another on our way downstream.

We would anchor for breakfast at Shotley, just out of the channel. The whole area is dominated now by the docks at Felixstowe with their huge cranes, and Shotley has a marina with a forest of masts to be seen above the river bank. Then there were marshes where the cranes now stand and the masts rise. The place was however not entirely quiet because Shotley was home to a naval training establishment, HMS Ganges, and breakfast could be taken to the sound of bugles summoning the cadets to their morning parade. Later in the day the mouth of the river would be criss-crossed by naval pinnaces in which the young men were taught the rudiments of boat-handling.

They were pleasant weekends, which the children seemed to enjoy almost as much as we did. Yet there was a thought which came to trouble me on each occasion. Sailing down to Shotley we would arrive at a bend in the river from which it was possible to look right out through Harwich Harbour to the open sea. This was the road to anywhere, yet so far every time we had passed the Harwich breakwater we had turned left or right along the coast. But across the water I was looking at, well below the horizon, were

Holland, Belgium and France. Could we not, one day soon, carry on, out of sight of land, and arrive at the other side of the North Sea?

I put the question to senior members of my yacht club, whose views I respected and who knew the type of boat I had. One of them looked hard at me for a moment and said: 'Well, in a boat like yours two or three fit and experienced men should not have too much trouble, but in your case ... No, I wouldn't try it.' I knew he was right. Successful as we had been in exploring the East Coast, this was a step too far. We needed more experience and a bigger boat. Both came sooner than I expected.

Our *deus ex machina* was Tom. Over the years several friends had sailed with me when Joy was too heavily engaged. I had been glad of their companionship and of their greater knowledge of the ways of the sea. Among them Tom was outstanding. He had a boat of his own which he sailed with his wife Brenda, his young son Matthew and, in those early days, a pug dog called Titus. Joy and I had joined them for short cruises and had absorbed as much as we could of Tom's seamanship. We never aspired to be his equals. No one we ever met was faster about the deck or calmer in a crisis.

The image which became part of the collective consciousness of my family is of Tom turning his pipe upside down as he went forward to change the foresail in a rough sea. He might return with his oilskins streaming with salt water but at least he kept his tobacco dry. Nor did his abilities stop at deckwork. He was an engineer and a skilled draughtsman who could design fittings for his boat, and even a complete boat if needed. And he could reduce navigation to its bare essentials, so that it became not a black art but a craft that I might learn to master. Only his eyesight had kept him out of the Navy, and that, I suspect, was the Navy's loss.

At the time I was beginning to look east, towards distant horizons, Tom had acquired a share in a commodious double-ender with a large diesel engine and a strong sea-going rig. 'Atlantis' was not a fast boat but was solid and thoroughly trustworthy. Joy and I were delighted when he invited us to be his crew on a crossing to

Holland where his family would join him for their summer holiday. We met at West Mersea and went aboard in the evening. Tom led me down to the small stern cabin. There was a chart clipped to the bulkhead, marked in places with fragments of Morse code, and a peculiar radio set with an instruction card fixed beside it. 'That', said Tom, 'is a radio direction finder. I've written all the call signs on the chart. Do learn how to use it, because you are the navigator. We sail at 09.00'.

The radio direction finder, or RDF as it was commonly called, was a fascinating piece of machinery. It was fundamentally a radio set with a cable leading to a stubby aerial on which was mounted a good quality compass. You tuned the radio to the frequency of a beacon marked on the chart and listened through headphones to the note it sent out. By turning the aerial this way and that you found the point at which the signal faded to insignificance. Then you knew that the compass was pointing towards the beacon. Of course it could equally well be pointing 180 degrees in the opposite direction, but if the rest of your navigation had been adequate there was rarely any doubt about which side of the beacon you were. After that you waited for another suitable beacon to transmit so that you could obtain a cross bearing.

If that sounds a trifle complicated, it was. That is even in the calm seas we had on that first voyage. What it was like in a near gale, when the boat was heaving about in all directions I was to discover later.

Mastering this new device while setting courses to allow for the tides sweeping up and down the North Sea, and updating our estimated position on the chart at regular intervals, certainly kept me busy. My first landfall was scarcely a triumph, because when the coast finally emerged from the mist the next morning, we were some three miles from where we had expected to be. Tom seemed pleased enough with the progress of his apprentice, but I was not entirely happy. Beneath my satisfaction in arriving safely at the other side of the North Sea lay a sense of disquiet.

In later years I came to accept such feelings as the natural lot of the navigator. Any navigator worthy of his or her chart table does not aim to be right within three miles or so: he aims to be right. Naturally this does not always happen, and when we are wrong there has to be an explanation. It is the search for such an explanation that builds a store of practical knowledge for use in future. All this seems straightforward now. At the time I hardly realised the commitment I was on the verge of making. At least the first step, to explain the error I had just made, was easy enough. I had misjudged the strength of the tidal stream out of the Schelde, as almost everyone does who is not familiar with that coast.

The chance to do better came the next year and again Tom was the instigator. He planned to sail to Calais with some friends and then westward down the English Channel. Joy and I were invited to join the crew for the first two stages. The voyage to Calais went smoothly enough, although entering the harbour in the dead of night stretched everyone's nerves a little. Since pushing our way into the yacht harbour at 04.00 might not have won us any friends, we moored to the commercial quay opposite and slept until it was time to visit the baker for our breakfast loaves.

The next day was spent in harbour. Tom's other two friends left to catch the ferry home and we rested while the wind from the west continued to rise. There was a large pile of sand at the far end of the quay some of which was picked up by the breeze and distributed over our decks and into the cockpit. We were too tired to appreciate the significance of this, beyond a certain gritty discomfort. It hardly seemed worth moving the boat, since we planned to leave early the next day.

The following morning found us on a swinging mooring in the Avant Port, waiting for the tide. The original intention had been to sail for Newhaven, but with an adverse wind it seemed that the short trip to Boulogne was more feasible. It was a grey, grim morning. 'Atlantis' rolled in the swell that came between the piers. When we finally set out it was to find a lumpy sea, worsening as the wind pushed against a strengthening tidal stream. More seriously, visibility was poor.

In most people's minds fog is not associated with high winds, and indeed it is quite rare to meet the two together, but it does happen. For it to occur when we had to beat down Channel, out into the path of ships crowding the Dover Straits and back towards cliffs we could not see, increased the anxiety level in all of us even in Tom himself. 'Atlantis' was not designed to sail close to the wind. Reefed down to cope with an incipient gale she lumbered through the peaks and troughs and made very little ground on each tack. Added to which she was not answering well to her rudder, to the point where Tom was having to start the engine to bring her round on to a fresh course.

Once a problem with the steering had been diagnosed, the cause was all too clear to us. The steering wheel was fixed to a bulkhead in the centre cockpit. From it wires ran through a series of sheaves on deck to the stern where they were attached to the rudder. The system was inherently imprecise because of the slack that could develop in those wires, but now the problem was the sheaves which had, unobserved by us, become clogged with sand. Clearly this was not the time to dismantle them and clean them out. Quantities of salt water were washing them from time to time, but this seemed to make things worse, rather than better. 'Atlantis' was in danger of becoming a lame duck.

For some hours we limped on, hoping to make Boulogne while the tide was still favourable. Once it turned however we had to contend with both wind and tide. Furthermore, although the waves might have been expected to subside under such conditions, these particular waves showed no inclination to do so. The fact was that the wind was still growing in strength, dousing all hopes of a flatter sea. It was time to put about and run for Calais.

Running for home did not of course solve our steering problems. Steering downwind is never easy, and with a rudder that answered reluctantly to the wheel great concentration was needed. Everything now seemed to be happening quickly. 'Atlantis' was rushing along with a bow wave almost up to her cockpit coaming. Navigation had to be speeded up accordingly.

I had only an approximate idea of the point at which we had turned, which did not help at all. With nothing in sight I had to rely on Tom's RDF set. It produced a bearing on Cap Griz Nez which showed us to be clear of the coast and safe for the time being, but we were too near the shore to obtain a reliable cross bearing to fix our position. This mattered because just in front of Calais is a sandbank which has to be avoided. To be carried too far north and swept on to it in the sea that was then running did not bear contemplation. The channel ran inshore of this and was marked by buoys. All we had to do was to find them.

Tom had now to rely on his navigator. 'For Pete's sake don't let me miss the CA3 buoy', he shouted down to me. Once sighted that would see us securely in the channel. I took another bearing on Cap Griz Nez and looked around for anything that would give me a cross bearing. Then for a few seconds the mist cleared to show a gleam of white from the shore – Cap Blanc Nez. A quick look at the compass, a mark made on the chart, a guess at the boat's speed over the ground, some mental arithmetic and I called up, 'Should be ahead in two or three minutes'. And in two and a half minutes it appeared ahead of us. Our roller coaster ride was soon at an end. We were back in Calais harbour after some ten hours at sea, getting nowhere but learning a lot.

If chance plays a part in our lives ashore, it does so even more at sea. I cannot count the times I have looked for a buoy that should be ahead and found it missing. That I got it right that time, when it mattered, was in large part due to luck. But the confidence it gave me changed my attitude to navigation completely. It was no longer a black art but something I could do.

From then on the task of navigating a small boat in all sorts of weather produced feelings of keen anticipation rather than of apprehension. Or if there was apprehension, as in the worst cases there must have been, it was outweighed by a compulsion to find, by any means available, the ship's position on the surface of the globe, and to set her on a safe course.

In those days there was no magical button to press to accomplish this, but there was a range of tools that could be used in various combinations. It started then, as it does now, with the chart. Charts have always seemed to me to offer a magic of their own. You may read them as you might a three dimensional book. They look down into the water, recording depth and the nature of the bottom of the sea. They look up to the land, showing the relative heights of hills or islands, the essence of the coastline, landmarks of all kinds. They allow you to recognise and identify buoys, lighthouses and harbour lights in daytime or at night. They show shipping lanes and frontiers, military zones, tidal streams, whirlpools and overfalls. Every country that produces them does so in a way that mirrors the needs of its mariners.

To supplement the charts there are pilot books with everything from weather information to harbour plans. They are of course written in different languages, but because they each adopt a routine format can usually be understood with the aid of the ship's dictionary. We used to buy them, along with the charts that we would need, early in the year, to plan our voyage, measure the distances involved and spot where the difficulties might lie. Some of the material had to be obtained from overseas. I recall taking a mini-cruise to Hamburg and spending the time ashore with Joy at a chart agent's office, returning to our cruise ship in a snow storm, laden with a great roll of charts.

Along with the chart your boat's main tool of navigation was, and still is, the compass. If it is sited as far as possible from magnetic influences, which can be anything from the engine to stray beer cans, it can give a fair indication of the earth's magnetic pole. Naturally the charts are based on the geographic pole and the position of magnetic north relative to this changes from place to place and from year to year. Charts always show this variation and proper navigators are taught to add or subtract it as appropriate each time a course is to be set. As a beginner this seemed to me to be asking for trouble: even the easiest sums can go wrong when you are tired, hungry and wet. The answer was a plotting device adjusted each day to allow for magnetic variation which made it possible to set courses on the chart without arithmetic.

Then we had the ship's log. This was at the time evolving from a propeller towed behind on a length of line to a small impeller fitted to the hull which revolved to measure both speed and distance run. It could however only show progress through the water, and the water might itself be moving under the influence of tide or wind. It was not therefore to be compared to a milometer in a car, and became particularly unreliable in choppy seas or if it got entangled with weed.

The echo sounder added a third dimension to navigation. It was often possible to use a depth sounding to check an estimated position, or even to sail along a depth contour marked on the chart. In tidal waters echo sounders had to be used in conjunction with tide tables to predict the depth of water at any given time and they were of little help where rocks rose sharply up from the sea bed.

Finally I could not resist the appeal of Tom's RDF system. Many yachtsmen at the time disparaged RDF, claiming that they could not obtain an accuracy better than 5° which was in most cases inadequate. This was partly because they used cheap equipment. The set which Tom had installed, a make which I subsequently bought for myself, was accurate to about 2° in almost any conditions. But there was a knack to using RDF. It required a good ear to listen to the signal and a steady hand. When challenged on the degree of accuracy obtainable, I would advocate regular exercise. When you could carry two pint mugs of beer, full to the brim, across a crowded bar room without spilling a drop, you were ready for RDF.

All these tools were useful, but none of them could be guaranteed to produce results on every occasion. Even the compass could be thrown out of gear by magnetic anomalies, usually caused by deposits of iron in the seabed, which were a feature of some of the northern waters we were to visit. So it was wise to treat navigation as a craft rather than a science. As with any craft, the skill lay in choosing the right tool to use at a given time, or even in inventing new tools when necessary. Aids not shown in instruction manuals included the rubbish trails left in times past by cross-channel ferries, the flight path of helicopters on their way to gas rigs, the sound of breakers or the song of birds on an unseen shore.

The ability to use the tools of navigation was to develop over the years ahead, as was Joy's skill as a helmswoman, taking charge of the boat while I sat at the chart table plotting the next course. At the time all we could do was imagine what the future might hold. Our small boat had no chart table. Furthermore, my friends in the yacht club had certainly been right. There was no way that the two of us, in our existing craft, would want to face the seas we had experienced in our adventures with Tom.

To see how this problem was solved we have to look again at life ashore. My parents had by now abandoned their mooring plot at Brundall and moved house to Norfolk, to live by the side of the River Bure. My father had retained his interest in the Broads and was active in the work of the Broads Society, a title which caused some amusement among his American friends. He had come with me on several short trips out to sea, but had remained true to his first love. Meanwhile I had prospered in my new job, but not to the extent of having money to spare for a new boat. With two children at school it was as much as we could do to maintain the boat we had.

My parents used to visit us from time to time and it was on one such visit that my father commented on the layout of my garden. The house had been built to one side of a sizeable plot in order to put space between us and the neighbouring pub. Paradoxically I had then built a small stile into the hedge bordering the pub in order to shorten the distance to the bar. Between our house and that hedge was a sea of grass that had to be cut frequently.

One afternoon, returning from the pub across the stile, my father remarked that land prices had recently risen sharply. Why not sell the grass and buy a bigger boat? A slightly longer walk to the pub would hardly matter, and I could then spend more time sailing and less on cutting grass. It cannot be said that the some such idea had never occurred to us but it had been seen as a long-term insurance for the future. We valued the space around our house but the need to expand our sailing range pressed hard upon us. So we took my father's advice and sold the land.

The boat we bought was called a Vega and made in Sweden. She was twenty seven feet long, with a long keel, a modern, masthead rig and a diesel engine. We called her 'Bugle' in honour of HMS Ganges and because she had a hull the colour of the small blue flower of that name. Now we had a boat fully capable of crossing the North Sea, which could also provide comfortable accommodation for all four of us on a summer cruise. I could even fit a portable chart table over the sink.

Our first steps were tentative enough. A crossing to Calais by the shortest of stages was followed by one to South Holland in the company of a more experienced friend. Then we got more ambitious. The passage from Harwich to Den Helder or the Frisian Islands was much longer but we could return in a series of day trips, some of them through inland waters, so nights at sea were rare. Yet over the next three years 'Bugle' travelled as far north as the German island of Borkum and as far west as Fowey. We were on a steep learning curve. But the further we went the further we wanted to go, and that brought us up hard against the problem of time.

I had obtained special permission to take all my summer holiday in one, but we still had to get back to our mooring at Woolverstone before I was due to return to the office. However we planned a cruise this limited the distance we could travel. Only the most foolhardy would rely on favourable weather for a long, overnight passage back home at the end of the holiday. The choice of risking either your job or your life did not appeal.

The answer was simple, although to a majority of British yachtsmen it was quite unthinkable. If the voyage home is a problem, just do not sail home. Leave the boat at the farthest point of the outward journey. Then all the time and mileage previously devoted to the return voyage can be spent going forward. Thus the cruising range can be extended without undue risk, and indeed, as it was in our case, largely by day-sailing.

There was a price to pay, which at first seemed daunting. It meant putting every scrap of leave together and taking the whole lot in one – no long weekends or short get-aways, and eleven months of boatlessness each year. It also required a good, reliable boatyard at the far end of each voyage, and a journey home by whatever public transport was available.

In time the obstacles fell into perspective. Boatyards were found which were just as reliable and no more expensive than those at home. We became expert in the railway timetables of Europe. It is true that the ability to escape for a weekend afloat was missed, but in compensation there was the excitement of planning next year's voyage and hunting down all the information needed to make it happen.

With our new plan of action came a change of boat. We sold 'Bugle' and bought another Vega, taking advantage of the manufacturer's efforts to obtain a larger share of the UK market. The idea was in part inspired by fear of the unknown. Since we would no longer be able to maintain the boat ourselves and would have to rely on untried boatyards, we hoped that starting with a new boat and largely new equipment would keep problems to a minimum. We named her 'Bunting', after the birds who inhabited the reedbeds of our early years and in anticipation of the courtesy flags she would be wearing in countries yet to be visited.

Our first target was Oxelösund on the east coast of Sweden. To get there meant rounding the long sweep of the Dutch and German Frisian Islands, passing through the Nord-Ostsee canal into the Baltic and finding our way through the dense archipelago which shelters the Swedish coast. In the time available this was quite an ambitious project for a family crew. The incessant need to press on while the weather allowed strained the patience of our two daughters, especially Katy's. She was then of an age to develop an agenda of her own, in which long days at sea did not rate highly. Neither she nor Helen accompanied us for two or three years afterwards, which was a pity because subsequent voyages were taken at a more leisurely pace.

This was possible because we were now established in a new and quite outstanding cruising area. Joy and I were alone for the next year's trip to Finland and the Åland Islands, a magical voyage during which the oilskins remained untouched in their locker and we were seduced into believing that the sun always shone in these parts. So it seemed in the following summer when we borrowed Tom's son Matthew to help us negotiate the numerous locks of the Göta canal right over Sweden to the Skaggerak, which we crossed to arrive on the much wilder west coast of Norway. 'Bunting' was left for the winter in Stavanger, while we discussed where to go next.

It was a long way back to England, whichever route we might choose, but Joy had another idea. As a west bound crow might fly Scotland is closer to Norway than is England. So why not go there? I was tempted but saw 266 reasons why not – the distance in sea miles between our eventual point of departure in Norway and Fraserburgh. For of course, we went.

Such a voyage meant two nights at sea and a more rigorous system of watch keeping than the rather casual one we had so far adopted. It also seemed to us to require a third crew member, to ensure that we all got enough sleep and to provide extra strength if the going should get rough. We persuaded Tom to join us, with the incentive of seeing something of Norway as we worked our way northward before taking our departure for Scotland. Sadly for him we almost immediately got a favourable wind which we all agreed could not be wasted.

A fine south-easterly breeze carried 'Bunting' all the way across the North Sea, to be met by dolphins off Kinnairds Head and escorted by them almost all the way into Fraserburgh. A favourable breeze also saw us right through the Caledonian canal to the west coast, where Tom caught a train home and we took a leisurely cruise to our winter mooring. We had intended to sail south in the spring, but our introduction to the western isles in that prolonged spell of fine weather tempted us to spend an extra year in the north, touring the outer islands. Thus it was that, cowering for days on end in the fishing harbour at Stornoway, we discovered what Scottish weather could really be like.

Firm plans were made to head south after that, taking a good look at Ireland on the way, but fate intervened to make this even more difficult than geography had intended. Joy fell ill and was out of action for a year or more. Eventually, after one false start and delays for gear box repairs, Tom once more came to the rescue. He and I sailed 'Bunting' to Falmouth, cruising along the east coast of Ireland in thick fog and seeing very little of it.

A base in Falmouth gave us the chance of making good that omission, once Joy had recovered sufficiently. We sailed out via the Scilly Isles and spent our summer holiday battling the west wind along the southern coast of Ireland, past the Fastnet Rock and into Bantry Bay before turning for home. But by then events ashore had taken a serious turn and the pattern of our lives was about to change. In the spring of the next year 'Bunting' was sailed to Lymington to be sold. She had logged nearly 6,000 miles in her long, slow circumnavigation of north west Europe, and had served us well.

The sale of 'Bunting' did not imply that we were turning away from the sea, quite the contrary, but to understand the decisions that had to be made it is necessary to look at two aspects of life ashore that were of inescapable importance. One of these centred on the house we had lived in for nearly twenty years; the other on the job I had been doing throughout this period, which had been our sole source of income.

It is, I suppose, common enough to see people you love as a permanent, unchangeable fixture, until suddenly they are old, and can no longer cope with the demands that age makes on them. This happened first to my mother, who became increasingly frail, to the point where my father felt he could no longer look after her in isolation. So we had an extension built on to our house to provide separate accommodation for the two of them. In the event my mother died just before they could move in, almost as if, in her quiet way, she wanted to avoid the fuss of moving house.

Thus it was that my father lived independently in his part of the house for the six years in which we were sailing 'Bunting' from country to country during our summer holidays. He took a lively interest in our travels, as he did in everything else. I believe it was a happy time for him: I know it was for us. When he died the house seemed very empty. I was then the only survivor of the family I had been born into and found that disturbing, a sad and irrevocable coming of age. In practical terms we now had a house larger than we needed, but there was also a feeling that the life we had enjoyed there was coming to an end.

That feeling was enhanced by uncertainty at work. My job had become insecure. After years of almost unbroken success the firm had fallen victim to the internal politics of the group to which it belonged. I was then fifty six. It might have been possible to stay on in some capacity or other in the hope of getting a full pension later, but that prospect was hardly attractive. Joy and I discussed the options open to us and decided that I should leave, take an early and much reduced pension, seek free-lance work in the winter time to supplement this, and spend the summer sailing. It was far from a risk-free strategy, but in our eyes at any rate, it had the merit of sanity.

To put the plan into effect we needed a new boat, one we could live in for perhaps three months in each year and which could carry the fuel, stores and spares necessary to give us a fair degree of independence. This could just be achieved by selling the house and buying a smaller one. Katy was by now married and Helen was spreading her wings, so there was no impediment to moving, although when the time came we all four felt the wrench keenly. Nor was it easy for Joy and I to find the house we wanted, but we did eventually discover one with a small, discreet walled garden that could be left to itself all summer.

The boat we had built for us was a Vancouver 28, designed

originally for ocean sailing, cutter rigged, well-ballasted – a boat for all weathers. There were only three berths because we expected to sail alone, apart from occasional visits by one or other of our daughters, or a friend. This gave the two of us ample space and provided me, at long last, with a magnificent chart table.

The tools of navigation arranged around that table now had two additions. We installed a Decca Navigator which could give us latitude and longitude at any time, and a Navtex receiver which would, somewhat erratically, print out weather forecasts in English. We had found radio forecasts difficult in northern waters. Quite apart from language problems, tuning in at the right time was bound to prove hard for a short-handed crew. Other things were always happening which demanded instant attention at that precise moment. And even if you made it to the set in time, taking a forecast down in writing was next to impossible for any but the nimblest fingers.

It was harder to feel good about the Decca. Push button navigation was not to my taste. To rely exclusively on an electrical device, itself dependent on the yacht's battery, seemed to me the height of folly. Nevertheless I had to admit that a reliable check on a position I had estimated by other means was often welcome, especially in fog, or when crossing shipping lanes or entering areas of magnetic anomaly, where the compass could not be trusted. So in time I grew fond of my Decca, although I used it mainly to mark positions on the chart, from which I would navigate much as I had always done. It was naturally far more accurate than my treasured RDF, which by then was being phased out, just as the shore-based Decca was eventually replaced by satellite navigation.

What we did not fit was VHF ship-to-shore or ship-to-ship radio. Acknowledging its potential use in an emergency, we still rejected it as an intrusion, an assault on the concept of independence which lay at the heart of our kind of sailing. I saw it as a means by which others would seek to control us, and I was of course right in this, although a lack of VHF did occasionally lead to some rather close encounters with frustrated officialdom in large, grey gunboats.

We could choose the colour of our new boat, and settled on a cream hull that reminded us of our first love 'Wild Rose'. I suppose we both suspected that, short of accidents, this boat would be our last. She was named 'Sea Bear', after a series of articles I had written for Yachting World some years before, and also because that was the name given to the fur seals that in time past had inhabited the Baltic. That our minds were set on another voyage north is abundantly clear.

'Sea Bear' was built at Itchenor, from where we sailed her on a proving cruise to France, and then to Holland with Katy, before laying up at Woolverstone to prepare for some years away from home. It was to be nine years in fact before she returned.

During that time we explored the tide-swept flats made famous by Erskine Childers in 'The Riddle of the Sands', wintering on the Schlei, where Davis and Carruthers went to shoot wild duck. We sailed the Eider river and the creeks of Jutland and wended our way through the Danish islands. We crossed to Norway and climbed up the canal that leads into the heart of Telemark, where Lake Bandak creates a deep inland fjord. We cruised through what had been East Germany in that heart-lifting time just after the Berlin wall had come down. Poland we visited twice, once while Communism reigned, supreme but weakening, and again when the harbour office was no longer guarded by a soldier with a sub-machine gun.

Finally, after several attempts when we had been frustrated by the northerlies that blow in the spring, we arrived at the very end of the Gulf of Bothnia, where the water is hardly salt at all, and the Arctic Circle is just up the road. Thus we came to meet many Swedes and Finns and to get to know harbours on both sides of the Gulf, and indeed all the way around the incredibly long coast of Sweden, from Haparandahamn in the north to Strömstad on the border with Norway.

By then 'Sea Bear' had become for us something of a magic carpet. We could set out one morning from one country and find ourselves the next day in a different culture altogether. She flitted from Sweden to Finland, from Denmark to Norway, from Poland to Sweden, from old regimes to new. Of course, at five knots it was a slow flit, and not all the voyages were without incident – some even offered a whiff of danger. Sometimes we would arrive very tired indeed. But we always trusted her to get us there. If it is possible for human beings to bond with a creature of wood, metal and plastic, then we and 'Sea Bear' were one.

It was with mixed feelings that we eventually turned south. Long ago, while we had wintered in Falmouth, we had entertained thoughts of an expedition in that direction, had dreamed of ocean passages across Biscay to the Azores or perhaps even to America. It was now too late for that. What we could do was what most British yachtsmen, at least those based on the south coast, do as a matter of course. That is, sail to the Channel Islands and to Brittany, places we had yet to see.

So we brought 'Sea Bear' back to Woolverstone and spent a winter bringing her back to new, or perhaps better then new, since the small modifications we made had the benefit of experience. Then we set off for France and worked our way around the coast to St.Malo, calling at Jersey on the way, along the rocky shores of Brittany, through the Chenal du Four and eventually into the Golfe de Morbihan.

'Sea Bear' spent the winter, comfortably enough, at Vannes, while we went home and took a hard look at ourselves and concluded that while she was still an all-weather boat, we were no longer an all-weather crew. Joy's legs were no longer reliable on deck while I had lost much of the strength in my shoulders. So in the spring we cruised south into the Bay of Biscay, as far as Les Sables d'Olonne, and then turned and made our slow way back, first to Guernsey and then across to Lymington. There Tom and Brenda met us to say goodbye to the boat and Helen joined us for a last sail before 'Sea Bear' returned to her makers at Itchenor to seek a new owner.

Looking back through our log books I have counted 1900 days that Joy and I spent afloat in one boat or another. That is over five years of our lives. In that time we sailed 26,500 miles, which would have taken us right round the world, had we chosen to go that way

– or been capable of it. If you divide one figure into the other you get an average of 14 miles a day. Of course there were many days when we did not sail at all, but spent the time working on the boat, waiting for better weather, or simply looking around and talking to the people we met. Nevertheless it was slow progress.

That is surely the way to travel. I see our boat as a small dot on the surface of the globe slowly, and sometimes painfully, clambering up parallels of latitude or sliding across meridians as she seeks out new ports and fresh experiences, and taking time to absorb them all into the fabric of her hull. A boat then is not a possession, rather a repository for dreams.

So the brief history of our travels I have sketched here is no more than a skeleton, the bare bones of memory. It would be a mistake to put chronological flesh on those bones, a day-by-day recital of the content of our log books. There were after all days when nothing happened that Joy or I would wish to remember. Besides, for us memories do not work in that way. They tend to band together, so you move from one to another as interest, not chronology dictates. So that, for instance, one night at sea may recall others of a very different kind.

This is a fairly untidy process, so I will try to group our memories in a reasonably coherent order, around the topics which most interested us. The history already given will have explained how our life afloat developed, and the events ashore which influenced it. To some extent that explains why we did what we did. Now I hope to show what made it all worthwhile.

CHAPTER THREE

The Lure of the North

A S EVERY READER OF 'THE WIND IN THE WILLOWS' KNOWS – and that must surely be every one of us – the Water Rat never went to sea. Yet he was sorely tempted to leave his riverside home. Listening to the Sea Rat's tales of ships and canvas and 'great green seas' he felt the pull of distant horizons. And that pull was always in one direction, southward. Fortunately the Mole caught him before he could leave, but when challenged about his intentions he made it quite clear that he had meant to go 'south, with the rest of them'.

What was it that made us head in the opposite direction? It was not sheer perversity, although it must be admitted that the idea of going anywhere at all 'with the rest of them' never held much appeal, either for Joy or for me. The south has always been a firm favourite, redolent of warmth, sun, friendly encounters with extrovert Latins, good food and wine. Whereas in our traditional wisdom the north is colder in every way, populated by solemn, humourless people, offering dull food at high prices. It cannot be said that, on these particular aspects at least, our own perceptions were very different before we set out.

Some of the most important choices we make are rational only in retrospect. True enough we have free will: the atoms of the mind swerve one way rather than another, and a decision is made. But we can choose only from what the mind already holds, and some of the concepts, aspirations or dreams it contains are sufficiently vague to be below the level of everyday consciousness, yet may exert a critical influence when their time comes.

The process which drew us to the north was an untidy one, that evolved in stages over some forty years. Its origins may have been in the armchair sailing of a schoolboy who spent the long summer holidays reading, with no thoughts of adventure beyond the pages of the books he devoured. Among these was a strange, in some ways rather clumsy, story of spies and plots among the Frisian Islands at the turn of the nineteenth century. 'The Riddle of the Sands' has come to hold a special place in the minds of yachtsmen, but of course, when I first read it I did not see myself as one of those. Nevertheless I was drawn into a world of sea and sand, where men of skill and courage battled with the elements, sailing a small boat with no engine, or rowed in thick fog to find their way through winding, tidal channels.

The book that Erskine Childers wrote is a love story. Forget Dollmann's daughter and the rather lame romantic interest said to have been added at the request of his publisher. The love that Childers depicts is a much more physical affair. It exists between him and the sands whose colour 'varied from light fawn, where the highest levels had dried in the wind, to brown or deep violet'; between him and his boat which the incoming tide had lifted off the sands and set afloat 'rocking easily and triumphantly'; between him and the spirit of adventure which inspired his book and ultimately brought about his death.

The schoolboy reading that book for the first time never for one moment saw himself in the role of either Davis or Carruthers, or even imagined that he would one day be navigating those convoluted channels. He simply absorbed the whole thing, sands, tides, boat, heroes and all into the deepest recesses of his mind, where it stayed bright and untarnished, so that when it emerged again it was as something almost tangible, waiting to be grasped.

It was inevitable that, as soon as we had a boat capable of crossing the North Sea, we should turn north towards Den Helder and the Dutch Frisian Islands, getting as far as Borkum, the first of the German chain, before lack of time forced us to turn back. And just as inevitable that in later years we should return to explore the other German islands and the channels between them. These are created by the tide rushing in between the islands and swirling around behind them. As it does so it slows and where the waters meet behind each island a watershed is formed, which may be crossed, even by a keel yacht, in the short period around high water.

It is this feature that made navigating these waters as fascinating for us as it had been for Davis and Carruthers. Timing is of the essence, as Erskine Childers makes clear in his account of the famous row in the fog from Norderney to Memmert. There was no way we could resist retracing the course his heroes were said to have taken, or wondering just how much of this tale was based on experience. It could certainly be done by two fit young men who got the tides just right, but sadly our own passage was not made under oars; neither was it in thick fog.

The withies that mark a safe route across the sands seem much as they must have been a century ago. Normally there is a single row of them, marking one side only of the channel. Pilotage, given an up-to-date chart, is not difficult except when visibility is poor. Our memory of the area is dominated by a day of motoring into a wicked wind and pouring rain, when the withies were hard to see and the risk of missing one and inadvertently cutting a corner was all too real. On a falling tide that would have left us high and dry for the rest of the day; but at least we would have been safe. Looking out to sea between the islands revealed a much more savage aspect of these waters. In these conditions the *Seegat* looked just as Childers describes his *Hohenhörn*, 'a wall of surf stretching across and on both sides'.

Indeed the sands, the sea, the surf and even the withies do not seem to have changed all that much since Childers wrote his book. But there have been other changes, which served to dent the impression of isolation and adventure I had carried in my mind. For our perils on that windy day came not from the villainous Dollmann, nor even from the weather itself; but rather from a steady procession of yachts and motor craft coming downwind towards us at high speed and hugging the same withies that we were using to find our way. They would loom suddenly out of the murk, to pass in a flash as we lumbered slowly on into the driving rain.

Happily all days were not like that. Life among the islands could be pleasant, even if the water had to be shared with more boats than Childers could ever have imagined. Indeed in some respects it was more civilised than in his time, since some of the small, coastal villages were no longer at the muddy end of tidal creeks, but closed off from the sea, so that you could lock through into a comfortable, sheltered basin.

Nevertheless, even on our first visit, the north was beckoning us to go further. Nature had thrown a barrier in our path, the peninsula of Jutland which separated the wilder waters of the German Bight from the tideless Baltic, and it was only natural that, faced with a barrier, we would want to get to the other side. Our curiosity had been sharpened by the habit British insurers had of covering yachts only within what they called the 'Brest/Elbe limits'. The fact that within these limits lurk some of the most dangerous waters in the world did not seem to worry them. What they were concerned about was the unknown and, however ludicrous it might seem to a European, for them what lay beyond Jutland was unknown territory. Which gave us an added incentive to go and see for ourselves what it was like.

Fortunately Kaiser Wilhelm II had made that easy for us, just as he had for Davies and Carruthers who travelled through his newly built canal soon after its completion (in 1895) and described it as a waterway that was 'broad and straight, massively embanked, lit by electricity at night till it is lighter than many a great London street'.

It was probably this description, coupled with the British habit of calling it, quite incorrectly, the 'Kiel Canal', that had given us to anticipate something vaguely industrial. The reality was much more rural. Of course the canal has had over a hundred years in which to mellow, but the countryside through which it passes is gentle and relaxed. The banks are still high, but there are a few places to stop where you can look out over what is predominantly dairy country. The cows are unmoved by the occasional convoys of large ships passing from one great sea to another. Once we even saw a deer come down the bank to the water's edge, to lighten a cold, rainy day.

On our first transit of the canal we had little time to spare for the surrounding countryside: what we wanted was to get to the other end. Just as children travelling to a seaside holiday strain their eyes to spot, beyond the houses and the trees, something that is unmistakably water, so we waited in anticipation as the great lock filled and we saw over the gates a sheet of the clearest blue. Gone were the greys of the River Elbe, the inky black of the canal itself; here was the Baltic, or at least the spur of it that tracks south towards Kiel. For an instant I was Xenophon hearing the joyous cries of his men, who had clambered right across Armenia, when they finally came in sight of 'The Sea, the Sea!'

It was indeed a significant moment for us, and one that would shape our sailing for years to come. For here the 'road to anywhere' I had first glimpsed looking out through piers of Lowestoft Harbour began to assume a specific direction. In reality there was a choice of directions in front of us once we had passed through those lock gates, north along the coast of Jutland or through the Danish islands to the west coast of Sweden or the mountains of Norway, east along the southern shore of the Baltic – although at that time most of that was still firmly in Communist hands – or north of east towards the Stockholm archipelago, the Åland Islands and Finland.

The simple act of traversing the Nord-Ostsee canal had opened a range of possibilities, and in the course of time we were to explore most of them in some depth. On that first voyage we had only one course to follow, around Sweden and then through the archipelagos of the east coast to Oxelösund.

What drove us in that direction was an impression we had gained from books and pictures of rocky, tree-clad islands set in a sea of blue. Oxelösund had been chosen as a destination because it was as far as we could reasonably expect to get in the time available

and because a member of my yacht club lived there and could recommend a boatyard to take care of our yacht in the ensuing winter. It was, after all, the first time we had steeled our nerves to leave
our boat overseas, and information on suitable places to do so was
extremely sparse.

Clearly, although the motivation to go north was strong, precisely where in the north did not then matter so much. What made
us return when we had more time and compelled us to go on
through the Stockholm archipelago and for hundreds of miles further into the Gulf of Bothnia was something much more powerful.
I suppose it could be said that our original motives were rooted in
images and aspirations. Later a certain degree of knowledge
entered the equation, and with knowledge the desire to learn more
about the places and people of a north that was more clearly
defined, and chosen as our own.

What strikes you first about the north is the light. It was a revelation to us, just as it has been to travellers for centuries past. It
seems certain that the bolder explorers of the Roman Empire got
as far as what is now Stockholm. Tacitus, writing in 98AD speaks of
the 'Suiones' possessing a civilisation based in the ocean itself, with
a fleet of double-ended, highly manoeuvrable ships. Looking further north into the Gulf of Bothnia he speaks of another sea, where
the last rays of the sun persist until dawn, bright enough to dim the
stars *(ut sidera hebetet)*. Indeed a crossing of the Gulf on a calm
midsummer night is an experience of rare intensity as the sun dips
below the horizon, only to rise again a short distance along, while
all the time a wide patch of blue illuminates the north.

Of course it would be far different in winter, but you would not
be sailing then because the water would be one large sheet of ice.
Naturally the people of the north react to these conditions by making the most of a summer that is all too short. They bask in the
bright sunshine for hours on end, stretched near naked on rocks
that reflect the warmth and glow golden in that clear light.

Then there are the islands themselves, hundreds of them, ranging from large rocks to tree-clad wildernesses capable of support-

ing a variety of wildlife, mink, beaver, deer or elk. Many of the people we met seldom sailed outside the archipelago. All they wanted was there. Their ideal was to find an island anchorage suitable for just one boat, so that they could have the place to themselves. To do this they had to pass outside the buoyed channels and enter areas where the depths were not well-charted and some rocks remained unmarked. Even quite close to Stockholm the chart reveals places like this, and our friend Leif Eklund, who lived on the island of Ingmarsö, made a business out of repairing motor boats which had damaged their propellers on what the Swedes called 'a little stone'.

Navigation through the islands, even along the recognised channels was, to use another Scandinavian euphemism, 'interesting'. Swedish charts are large-scale but cut into a size which enables them to be handled in the cockpit. Even at five knots you might have little time to decide whether to leave an island to port or starboard. To a stranger the islands all look remarkably similar, all low-lying and covered with trees. The channel markers were often very small and hard to recognise against the sun.

For us this was a new kind of sailing, very different from a brisk passage on the open sea, preferably followed by a visit to a waterside pub. It took time to adjust, and to accept that for us a voyage through the islands was likely to be nerve-wracking and tiring, with no pub at the end of the day. Somehow we became more reconciled to all this when, in 'Sea Bear', we had hit our first 'little stone'. To our delight the boat climbed gently over it, and slid safely down the other side. Her keel configuration might have been designed specifically for northern waters.

Apart from passages through the archipelago it might be thought that navigation in those tideless waters would hold little fascination for someone weaned on Admiralty Tide Tables. Indeed we did miss the help that tidal streams can lend to a well-planned voyage, although in return we were relieved of the need to sail in the cold light of dawn to catch them. But those tideless seas had lessons to teach us that we could not easily have learned at home.

Water levels may not have shown any tidal influence, but in

practice they varied with barometric pressure and under the influence of a prolonged blow from a settled direction. The difference could in some circumstances be as much as a metre. This meant that if you had the misfortune to go aground it was wise to get off as soon as possible. No rising tide would come to your rescue and if the level fell you could be there for a very long time. Such occasions saw the pair of us hanging over the bow and rocking the boat in an attempt to lift the deepest part of the keel so that the motor could pull us off stern first – not elegant, but it worked.

Winds could bring about other effects which could prove disconcerting. Initially these took us by surprise because of their apparent randomness. For example, quite strong currents could be met in the narrow straits between islands. On reflection it was clear that these were wind-driven. That this effect was sometimes part of a wider pattern became known to us during our second summer in the north.

After wintering in Oxelösund we decided to spend our holiday exploring the Åland Islands and the Finnish coast beyond them. With little time and the likelihood of having to face westerly winds on our way back we reverted to our old habit of a long leg outward bound and a return in smaller steps. This meant an open sea passage to one of the few safe entry points between the Finnish islands.

The intention was to sail from Sandhamn out of the Swedish archipelago and to enter Finnish waters by rounding the island of Utö, some ninety miles away. On Utö there was a conspicuous lighthouse to serve as a landmark, but the chart also indicated a problem. To the west of Utö lay the Svartbådan shoals, and between them and us lay a large area of magnetic anomaly. That meant that we would not be able to rely on our compass. Even if we had Utö in sight we could not be sure of its direction from us, and thus be certain that we were clear of those shoals.

On later voyages, equipped with Decca, this would have been a minor problem. We would have known the extent of any compass error and would have been able to correct our course accordingly. As it was we had to devise a plan to keep us clear of any hazards. It happened that about three miles south of Utö there was another lighthouse, Lillharun. What I intended to do was to keep Utö ahead until Lillharun was visible, then make for that to keep us away from any shoals.

For a whole day all went well. The wind remained steadfastly west of south, so that we could sail in warm sunshine with a fine breeze abaft the beam. By evening however it was clear that 'Bunting' was going too fast if we wanted to avoid entering the Finnish archipelago in darkness. I dropped the foresail and ran on under our small mainsail, which slowed progress to about four knots. But it was still dark, or rather a luminous shade of grey as we headed for the bright light on Utö and looked for the red flashes of Lillharun.

Utö soon became worryingly brilliant and seemed higher above the horizon, but Lillharun just would not show itself. Eventually I spotted an irregular light on the starboard bow and called Joy to the cockpit to help identify it. It could have been Lillharun with its light obscured by the odd high wave, but it did not look red. In a few minutes it became clear that this was not Lillharun but the small light on the Svartbådan rocks close up. We were now on the wrong side of the rocks and standing into danger.

I had been using a smaller scale chart to cover the open sea between Sweden and Finland. Now Joy fetched the large scale chart covering Utö and the Svartbådan shoals into the cockpit. It showed a way through the rocks which in calm weather and daylight would have been quite safe. In the hazy grey around us then and in waves five or six feet high I did not fancy our chances. We started the motor and with its help went back the way we had come, plugging into a steep, wet sea, until it was possible to clear Svartbådan on its safe side. We passed within two miles of Lillharun but saw neither the light nor the lighthouse itself.

By now something like a genuine dawn was breaking. Full sail was hoisted once again for the fifty mile run to Turku through the islands. Some of these were large and the channels between them wide, quite unlike the Stockholm archipelago. The land was obviously inhabited, but very sparsely. For the first five or six hours the rocks and the trees stared back at us but nothing moved, either on land or water. It was a weird experience, amplified by the tiredness that came over us after our encounter with Svartbådan.

As the sun grew warmer a coaster came chugging up behind us. She was a British ship and, seeing our red ensign, the officer of the watch leaned out from his bridge to wave as he passed. After that traffic gradually became thicker until we were able to turn off the main channel in the early afternoon and enter the yacht harbour of Ruissalo. There, moored between posts and the shore, we were free to enjoy the sleep we badly needed. To our delight the harbour was surrounded by reed beds and as I was dozing off I thought I heard a reed bunting twittering among them.

Over the next day or two I thought hard about what had happened to give us such a scare. It was no use blaming Lillharun. We should never have been on the wrong side of the Svartbådan shoals. On reflection I decided that we had paid too much attention to the magnetic anomaly – a novelty for us – and too little to the more predictable effects of the weather.

The fact that it had been blowing steadily from the south for some days should have warned me. Instead it gave me a false sense of security, leading me to expect no surprises. Indeed there was nothing visible to give cause for apprehension. With a fair wind the boat seemed to be running true, making very little leeway. But what I now suspected was that the whole surface of the sea, under the influence of that wind, had been drifting very slowly northward. At only a quarter of a knot that would, over twelve hours, have put us three miles north of where we believed we were. My safety margin had been quite inadequate to cope with this.

By now I was developing a more healthy respect for tideless waters, and the lessons they had to teach. If the problem had indeed been surface drift, that could, of course, occur anywhere, but might not be recognised as such in tidal areas. The tendency there would have been to assume that you had merely misjudged the strength of the tidal stream, as indeed you would have done.

So to the attraction of bountiful light and the ever-changing aspect of islands could be added the fascination of navigating these often deceptive waters. However it needed more than these factors to bring us back and set us on course towards the northernmost end of the Gulf of Bothnia. At the heart of it was curiosity, curiosity about the place itself, about the people who lived there and about the history which had shaped their lives in the past and was continuing to do so now.

In general the British seemed to know about as much as the ancient Romans of anything beyond Stockholm and the Åland Islands. The few yachtsmen who had sailed that far north had generally turned right at Stockholm and headed for the Gulf of Finland or the Baltic States. In doing so they were following a well-established historical pattern.

Before the Cape was rounded or the New World discovered there were two great trade routes along which goods from the east reached western Europe. One was through the Mediterranean, the other followed the Russian rivers northwards then crossed the Baltic to Sweden and Germany. The Hanseatic towns of Visby, Kalmar, Stralsund and Hamburg marked its progress, but goods and people had travelled this route from time immemorial. With easier access to Russia and the Baltic States it seems ever more likely that leisure sailors will continue in this tradition.

It is not only British yachtsmen who take this option and ignore the waters to the north. Even among Swedish sailors it is comparatively few who venture farther than the northern extremity of the Stockholm archipelago. As one of our friends who lives in Sundsvall said, 'For Stockholm sailors to go beyond Öregrund is like falling off the edge of the world'. They have less excuse than Tacitus, who believed that the Gulf of Bothnia was an arm of the Ocean encircling our earth, but it is possible to see why if you stand on the harbour wall at Öregrund and look north. On either side the land falls away until you are gazing at a flat horizon, devoid of islands or any sign of life.

What lay before us was a huge stretch of water. Most atlases and charts made it seem even greater than it is, because of the distortion caused by projecting the globe on to a flat surface. This has the effect of lengthening the apparent distance between parallels of latitude as you go north. So the distances may not be as much as they appear on paper, but they are still formidable. From Öregrund to Haparanda where the gulf ends is some 370 sea miles, while Vaasa, still a long way short of the end, is 200 miles away.

In imagination we can see the early Swedes exploring this great gulf and discovering that, regardless of what Tacitus had to say, it did indeed have an end. In their minds they had arrived at the extremity of an enormous creek which started just north of the Stockholm area, where their civilisation had its base. They called it simply 'The Bottom', for that is the meaning of the Swedish word *Botten*, which became in medieval Latin 'Bothnia'.

The Swedish side of the Gulf is fairly straightforward, just millions upon millions of conifer trees, until you reach the High Coast. This term is comparative, since the ground rises to little more than 200 metres, but this produces a sailing paradise. Instead of an archipelago there are a number of offshore islands of differing heights. Although the High Coast is no more than 50 miles long it provides a variety of channels and harbours that make it a marvellous cruising ground, vaguely reminiscent of the Western Isles of Scotland, but with more civilised amenities.

The Finnish coast is altogether more difficult. Here are not the large islands and wide channels of the south of Finland. Apart from the extensive and intricate archipelago around Vaasa, you are faced with a random scattering of isolated rocks stretching for miles offshore. It requires care to thread a way through these to the main harbours of this fascinating country.

At the bottom of the Gulf is yet another archipelago, shared between Sweden and Finland, where the waters are hardly salt at all and the islands are rimmed by boulders brought down by glaciers before history began. Here, if you set sail early in June, patches of fog can be seen on the horizon, marking places where the ice is still melting.

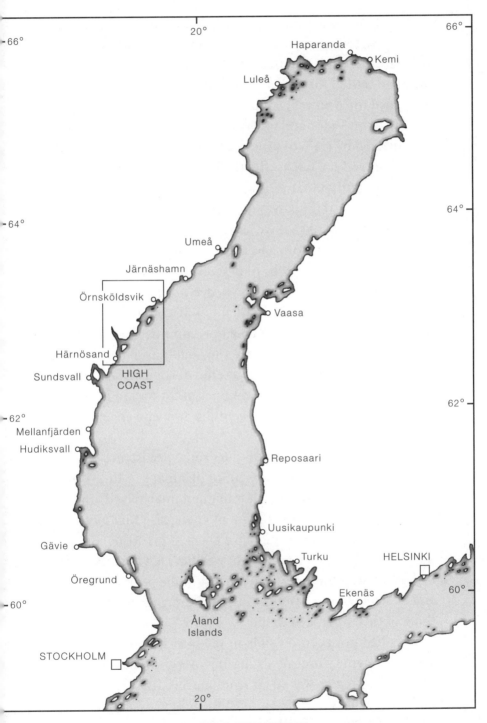

THE GULF OF BOTHNIA

It took us some time to get to the bottom, because at our first attempt we found the wind blowing from the north in the spring, and with the certainty that it would turn into the south for the summer, settled for a visit to the High Coast. Something similar happened the next year, although we did make a thorough exploration of the Vaasa archipelago before crossing to Umeå, where Katy arrived by train to join us for her summer holiday. We were able to introduce her to the delights of the High Coast before retreating south once more and abandoning the Gulf for a year. It was clear that a rethink was needed.

The problem was that we had been trying to do it all, there and back, in one season from a base in the south. The answer had to be a boatyard in the far north. To find one was not easy. The distances between towns in that part of Sweden are considerable and each separate community is remarkably self-contained. Our friends in Stockholm were quite unable to recommend a place to winter in the north because of course they had never wanted to do so themselves. Eventually through a series of contacts we found a yard in Luleå and later a superbly equipped yacht station in Båtskärsnäs even farther north, so that we were able to spend an entire summer at the bottom of the Gulf.

To return for a third time argues some persistence on our part. There may have been an element of obstinacy in this. We had set ourselves an objective which remained unachieved, and no one likes to be beaten, especially in an enterprise that any seasoned hell-for-leather sailor would have taken in his stride. But we were not sailors of that sort, and might well have left the task unfinished had it not been for a growing interest in the people of that region and a feeling that we were at last beginning to understand something of their approach to life.

This had not been possible in the busy harbours of the south. There anonymity prevailed. Sharing overcrowded moorings with complete strangers was so far from the Swedish ideal that most of our fellow sailors retreated into polite reticence and so became very like the stereotyped Swedes we had been led to expect.

Once past Stockholm all this changed. Partly it was a matter of simple arithmetic. Harbours were smaller and visitors fewer, so that they became objects of some curiosity, rather than tourists to be processed and sent on their way. One imagines that this phenomenon would be experienced anywhere in the world by anyone passing beyond the ever-expanding tourist sphere. Yet the welcome we received had a flavour all its own.

Our memories linger on Mellanfjärden and on Midsummer. Mellanfjärden is a small harbour at the head of a sheltered creek south of Sundsvall. We found the place with some difficulty because the entrance is hard to identify from the sea. Unknown to us it was also the destination that local yachting families had chosen for their Midsummer celebrations. The harbour was as crowded as anywhere we had been, but here was no anonymity. As soon as we stepped ashore we were welcomed by Göran, who had organised the rally, and invited to join in.

Mellanfjärden was blessed with a restaurant overlooking the water, where we ate and drank into the small hours. There is a certain vagueness to my memory of conversations after midnight. Even the Swedes, who are early risers, were slow to start on the following morning, but they had organised a wonderful post-hangover event. This was a treasure hunt, with clues hung from trees along a trail which eventually lead to the beach. Our difficulty was not just that the clues were written in Swedish. The local mosquitoes had discovered that trees with clues suspended from them were a prime source of nourishment. They surrounded each such tree in a dense cloud and made participation in the treasure hunt a test of courage and endurance.

The hunt ended with a party on the beach. There was a barbecue and prizes for everyone, even English visitors who had done nothing to deserve them except perhaps braving the mosquitoes. Above all, there were songs, sung to an accordion which was passed from one player to another. Then we strolled in company back to the harbour, all to sail our different ways. For our Swedish companions this was one more Midsummer to remember. For us it was a new experience, with a unique atmosphere.

Just what is it that makes Midsummer so special? This was not the only Midsummer we were to witness, although it did define the experience for us. Not all that happens at Midsummer is so innocent, any more than are our own Christmas celebrations. But, just as we cherish an unattainable ideal of what Christmas might or should be, so the people of the north know exactly what Midsummer is all about.

It is a time of light, of romance, of garlands and of simplicity. Flowers are everywhere, boats are decorated with greenery, young girls wear garlands on their heads and dance around a festooned pole, the 'Midsummer Stone'. Even dogs are seen wearing a collar of flowers. Swedes often marry at Midsummer, as it is considered particularly auspicious to do so. They drink, they sing and talk very openly with each other. The pretentious or hide-bound would surely feel out of place here.

To us these celebrations seemed untouched by modernity, unless the accordion is considered modern. Initially we seemed to be back in the earlier part of the twentieth century, but of course the whole idea is more ancient than that. In translating *De Rerum Natura* I came across a passage in which Lucretius describes the development of music and the music making activities of primitive humans.

'These tunes would soothe their minds and delight them after a good meal. For at such times simple pleasures are taken to heart. They would talk and joke and laugh merrily together, for then the rustic muse was in full vigour. Their playful mirth led them to adorn head and shoulders with leaves and flowers, and to dance, ... stamping the earth with heavy feet, smiling and laughing cheerfully at their efforts. For all these things were fresher then and more full of wonder.'

Lucretius would be delighted to see what he thought had passed away in prehistory still alive today. These things remain fresh and full of wonder, in Sweden. And he would also rejoice at a celebration which has escaped the fate of our winter and spring festivals and avoided annexation by religion. Midsummer stands alone in this, possibly pagan, but firmly human.

Naturally enough we took the enthusiasm with which people in the north greet Midsummer to be a reaction to the prolonged gloom of winter. I am not sure that we were entirely right. It is true that winter starts early, especially at the bottom of the Gulf, where we have experienced heavy frosts in September. Nor does it easily relax its grip; the ice may not disperse until late May or June. But Swedes do not go into hibernation and sleep the winter away.

In some years the ice might extend as far south as Stockholm, when our friend Lars could skate out along the channels of the archipelago to an island of his choice. A 'green' winter, when the ice did not form, was a disappointment.

There was no risk of that in the northern archipelago. Winters there meant snow and ice and long hours of darkness. Yet life went on, and not always in centrally heated, triple glazed buildings. As autumn approached people could be seen practising for cross-country skiing, while Ulf, an experienced sailor with whom we stayed in Lövskär, near Luleå, was busy adjusting compasses on snow-scooters.

Initially we had no idea how many of these machines there were. By the time we arrived for the summer sailing season not a single one was to be seen. We had however been puzzled to find a number of small sheds around yacht harbours in the area of Luleå, sheds too small to house a car. It seemed that the Swedish love of islands was a year-round obsession. In summer they sailed out to them by boat; in winter they rode out to them on snow-scooters. Those who had a summer house on an island could, if they wished, spend Christmas there, warming themselves by log fires.

Apart from such activities life continued through the winter much as it did elsewhere. People in the north had to earn and to spend, to educate themselves and their children, to sing in choirs and to play winter sports. Marriages sometimes came under pressure, so that when we returned in the next spring we occasionally found old friends with new partners, but it seems doubtful if the long dark winter could take all the credit for that.

What was clear was the passion with which the return of the sun was greeted. Lives were not lived at a uniform pace, in a dull, grey haze. Nor was it a matter of black and white, more of a star-studded indigo, followed by a blaze of vivid colour. People who live like that are aware of the shortness of life, and of the need to live it to the full.

In the harbour of Sundsvall there is a public quay used by boats to take on water and fuel. It is not a romantic spot. 'Sea Bear' lay there one morning, preparing for the next stage of her journey north. Astern of her was a Swedish yacht with two young men aboard, who invited us to join them for coffee. They then produced a guitar and launched into a series of delightful songs. At least they seemed delightful, although we could not understand the words. We asked what the songs were about and were told, 'About summer, and about love.' What else should we have expected?

'Wild Rose' on
Oulton Broad.
Picture by Ford Jenkins

Katy learns the ropes.
Picture by Ford Jenkins

'and took a swinging mooring on the River Orwell'

Pin Mill in 1972

'Bugle' newly arrived at Woolverstone

Joy steers 'Bugle' past the Shivering Sands

Helen keeps
a lookout, off
Walcheren

The Van
Harinxma canal
at Leeuwarden

Gripsholm Castle from the moorings on Lake Mälar

Kalmar Sund, approaching the bridge to Öland

'Bunting' at Näsby in the Finnish islands

A 'staircase' of locks on the Göta canal at Berg

The Lysefjord near Stavanger

Oil rig under tow in the Moray Firth

Tobermory, on
the way to meet
our otter

The Fastnet Rock on
a rare fine day

CHAPTER FOUR

Of Graveyards and Memorials

T HE NEXT SET OF MEMORIES serves to add another dimension to our journey northward. We live in the present and greet the people we meet on our travels as they stand, in the here and now. But Germans, Finns and Swedes are not Englishmen who happen to speak another language. The way they see the world has been shaped by a history very different from ours. If we are to understand them better, it is as well to know something of that history, and especially of the events of recent years, the essence of which will have been conveyed to them directly by their parents or grandparents.

Such knowledge as we gathered was not obtained by incorporating into our cruise planning a study of Scandinavian or Finnish history. To do so would not have been easy, since good books on these subjects written in, or translated into English were difficult to obtain. Nor would it have been strictly necessary, for much of this history is in full view of the traveller, written on the headstones of graves or displayed on memorials for all to see.

We first realised this on one of our earlier cruises to Holland. Hindeloopen is a harbour on the eastern shore of the Ijsselmeer. Because it lay close to the industrial heartland of Europe many German as well as Dutch yachtsmen kept their boats there. The village itself was quite small, with little for weather-bound sailors to do, beyond strolling around the church, with its quaintly tilted steeple. There, in the churchyard, we found the graves of several British airmen, who had crashed into the sea during the 1939-45 war, and whose bodies had been recovered when the water had been drained to make new polders.

At the time it felt strange to be walking there in company with Germans whose fathers may have occupied this land during the war or have fought with these airmen in the skies above the Ijsselmeer. But that was our insularity speaking. To European eyes we were standing at one end of a great plain which stretched from the Low Countries all the way through Germany and Poland, right up to the gates of Moscow. For centuries armies had moved over this plain, first one way and then another, while millions of ordinary folk had trudged the roads as refugees, leaving their homes behind them.

The suffering that this has caused reached a peak in the last century. One aspect of this was made clear to us by a memorial in the churchyard at Arnis. Arnis was our base for exploring German and Danish waters in 'Sea Bear'. It is on the Schlei, set in quiet countryside, inhabited by people who are seldom seen to hurry, but pursue life at their own cheerful, gentle pace. A more peaceful spot would be hard to find.

The memorial resembled those found in many English villages. It contained the names of the dead of two great wars. There was however a significant difference. Invariably such memorials show two columns of names, one for those killed in the 1914-18 war and one for the 1939-45 conflict, and always in England the list for 1914-18 is longer, usually far longer. Not so in Germany. In Arnis the 1914-18 names occupied one column: those for 1939-45 filled two columns. The shock to me was the preponderance of dead from the last, more recent war. The reason for this has to be the massive losses suffered on the Russian front. There is no doubt that the Germans have paid a heavy price for the military adventures of their leaders.

Their awareness of this became even clearer on a visit we paid to the harbour of Laboe. This small seaside town in Kieler Förde is dominated by the tall 'Marine-Ehrenmal', a naval monument shaped something like the conning tower of a submarine. The moment you enter, you are faced with the stark statistics of naval personnel killed in the two wars: '1914-18: 35,000, 1939-45: 120,000'. This of course was not on the Russian front, but in the cold waters of the Atlantic.

On the walls beside these bare figures are the silhouettes of the ships that were sunk. In the last war that included 840 U-boats. Elsewhere there is displayed the tonnage of the shipping which these, in their turn, destroyed. Clearly these figures are meant to speak for themselves. They certainly did to Joy, for hidden among them was an older brother who had served in the merchant navy and had never come home, torpedoed somewhere off the Western Approaches.

It took a shift in perception to see all this through German eyes. We had spent our childhood on an island besieged by an unseen enemy, lurking to pounce on unarmed merchantmen. The men who manned the U-boats were treacherous killers, of whom nothing good could be said. To the Germans they were heroes who suffered untold hardships beneath the waters, away from home for months at a time, as often as not never to return.

The monument at Laboe makes it easier to reconcile these very different views. In the basement is the dimly-lit Weihehalle where the names of the dead are inscribed and unit flags displayed. It is intended to be a place of sorrow and reflection rather than of triumph. There is pride here, but not arrogance.

After the Weihehalle it was a relief to come across a reconstruction of the Battle of Jutland, which was fought in 1916. If history has a lighter side it must lie in the ironies and ambiguities it throws up. This again is mainly a matter of perception, or of who writes the history. In most English accounts the Battle of Jutland was a great British victory that kept the German fleet out of the North Sea. In Laboe it was also seen as a victory, but a German one that kept the British out of the Skagerrak.

The ability of whole populations to close one eye is not confined to Britain or Germany. We were to find evidence that the Swedes were not immune to it as we went deeper into the Gulf of Bothnia. Swedish history has followed a very different course from ours or that of the Germans. The Swedes had embarked on a short-lived period of militarism in the seventeenth century, when Swedish kings had come to rule not only Finland but large parts of the southern shore of the Baltic. Then, faced with the growing power of Russia, and later of a united Germany, Sweden had withdrawn into its shell and adopted a posture of armed neutrality.

This process had not been entirely painless. In Ratan, a natural harbour well on the way to the north of the Gulf, we found the graves of two Swedes who had fallen when the Russians attacked the place in 1809. The conflict was brief and the casualties few, at least among the military, although the village had suffered in the bombardment that had accompanied the rather scrappy action. The Swedes counted it a victory: they had driven the Russians away. It is however noticeable that from 1809 Russia assumed control of Finland, which had been a Swedish domain for many years.

Swedish neutrality ensured that they suffered no casualties at all in the great wars of the last century. Swedes are not keen to talk about their actions in the second of these wars. They kept Hitler supplied with iron ore from their mines in the north. With the German army in charge of Denmark and Norway, and Finland under German influence, it is hard to see what else they could have done. To prosper while others suffer may be a source of unease, but is of itself no reason to bring down suffering on your own citizens. And Swedish neutrality did provide a discreet haven for refugees from the countries which had been occupied.

The Cold War put the policy of armed neutrality under stress once more, and in a way which was to impinge directly upon us as we sailed 'Sea Bear' through Swedish waters. The Swedes have always seen the screen of islands which fringes so much of their coastline not just as a playground but also as a natural defence against invaders. The fact that this *skärgård* had not proved particularly effective in the past did not deter them. They established within it a number of restricted areas and patrolled them with gunboats, camouflaged to merge with the rocks and the trees.

On our first visit we had found everyone fairly relaxed about such areas and had sailed through them blissfully unaware of the detailed regulations which governed the movements of foreign vessels within them. Then in October 1981 all this changed.

The cause was a navigational error on the part of a Russian submarine which happened, for no respectable reason, to be exploring the southern archipelago. The skipper failed to read his charts correctly and ran aground near the naval base of Karlskrona. To make matters worse, it was not the Swedish Navy which discovered this, but some local fishermen. There was of course a public outcry and the cartoonists in the press did nothing to soothe the wounded pride of the military. The fuss went beyond the usual political opportunism that normally attends incidents of this kind. The Swedes really felt that their natural defences had been breached and that something would have to be done about it.

To make matters worse, in February 1986 an event occurred which, though quite unconnected, did even more to create an atmosphere of insecurity. The Prime Minister, Olaf Palme, was shot dead in a Stockholm street while strolling innocently along with his wife. It is hard for an Englishman to comprehend the impact of this event in Sweden. We have come to accept that attempts will be made on the lives of our Prime Ministers: the risk is part of the job. The Swedish public at this time was far less inured to violence, and less cynical about the nature of the polity which had been developed over many years of peace. Now the uncertainties and dangers of the world outside had appeared on the streets of their own capital.

The significance of this recent history had not registered with us when, in 1988, after a long day's sailing, we sought an anchorage for the night off the island of Tärnö in the southern archipelago. Our chart seemed to place us in a 'semi-restricted' zone, marked with an anchor symbol, so we assumed that a short stay was permitted. Some local yachtsmen did not agree, and I made the mistake of arguing with them. The upshot was that, in failing light and at an obligatory four knots, we were escorted by a patrol boat into the harbour at Karlshamn. There we were visited by a huge policeman who seemed to fill 'Sea Bear's' cabin. He produced a booklet showing the authorised anchorages, which did not correspond wholly with those on the navigational chart. It seemed that the anchor symbol I had chosen was for Swedes only. Apparently a similar booklet was available for each restricted area, obtainable locally; which meant that a visitor from overseas might well have transgressed before he got one.

The incident was embarrassing and served to remind us that we were indeed foreigners, with a very different set of attitudes towards officialdom and regulations from those of the Swedes of Tärnö. We did however take it to heart, so that on our arrival at Härnösand in the Gulf, we went along to the police station before entering the local restricted zone. Again a booklet was produced for our enlightenment, but no one seemed to care much where we were going. The people of the north are, it seemed, more trusting.

If Swedish prosperity has been founded on a jealously guarded neutrality and on years of peace, that of Finland has been achieved by much harsher means. The incidents I have recounted to explain Swedish attitudes in recent years would have seemed insignificant to a Finn. The last century in Finland has been marked by violence and drastic changes in fortune. Nevertheless to see what might lie behind the Finnish outlook it is desirable to go further back in time.

While the early Swedes, or Suiones, were building something like a civilisation in the area that is now Stockholm, life in Finland seems to have been more primitive. Tacitus speaks of a tribe he calls the Fenni, who he says lived in a state of astonishing savagery and disgusting poverty *(mira feritas, foeda paupertas)*. He may, as some think, have been talking about the Lapps, but the Latin name caught the imagination of the Finns and has been used by them as a mark of national identity. In any event the description reminds us that for many centuries the life of a Finnish peasant was to be almost as hard as he implies. The current prosperity of Finland is of very recent origin.

Because of its location on the fringe of civilisation Finland was never so structured a feudal society as the rest of Europe became in the early Middle Ages. Feudal relationships depended upon the ownership of land in fixed locations. Finnish peasants could, and for many generations did, move to another part of the forest, cut themselves a clearing for a few crops, hunt in the surrounding area, and move to a new place when the land was exhausted, or when someone more powerful demanded tribute from them.

This may have helped to establish a tradition of sturdy independence in individual Finns; it did nothing to promote the independence of the Finnish nation. Caught between Sweden and Russia, Finland would inevitably fall under the influence of one or the other.

The Swedes ruled most of the country for most of the time until 1809, with Turku (or Åbo as it is in Swedish) as the capital. Swedish is still the language of many living in the south-western coastal strip, as it is of the Åland islanders. Nevertheless with the rise of Russian power and the eclipse of Swedish militarism in the early eighteenth century, Finland came increasingly into the Russian sphere of influence. It was unlikely after the establishment of St. Petersburg as a capital looking towards the west that any Czar would tolerate a frontier too near his most important city. Eventually this led to the conflict of 1809 and to the incorporation of Finland into the Russian empire.

It may be that this is the point at which the development of modern Finland began. For centuries the Swedes had been the ruling class and Swedish the official language. Russian rule was originally much more relaxed. Finland was an autonomous state, a Grand Duchy with the Czar as the Grand Duke: it was not a province of Russia. Although Swedish was still the language of the educated classes, change began after Helsinki was made the capital in 1812. By 1863 an edict was in place giving the Finnish tongue equal status in official dealings with the public.

The relationship between the Czar and his Finnish subjects had been strengthened by the appearance of a foreign enemy, the British. The so-called Crimean War began in 1854 with an expedition to the Baltic made by a combined British and French fleet. Finding the Russian naval base at Kronstadt too well defended, the fleet turned its attention to Finland. At Bomarsund, in the Åland Islands there was a Russian fort, quite newly built but of an obsolete design, with a garrison of 2,300 men and only 66 guns in place and ready to fire, no match for the 12,000 men and powerful ships ranged against them. The fortress was destroyed and most of the garrison taken prisoner.

When we visited the site in 1980 there was not much to be seen but, however futile the affair had been, it was impossible not to admire the navigational skill which had taken those huge, clumsy ships through the narrow, rock-strewn channels to put them in a position to bombard the unfortunate Russians.

Several years later we discovered more evidence of that ill-conceived naval expedition. Apparently the British fleet went on to attack the Finnish coast much farther to the north. That of course brought them up against the nature of that shore of the Gulf of Bothnia, with its shallow waters and isolated rocks. Undeterred, they lowered the ship's boats, fitted a small cannon in the bow and sent them towards the distant shore. The Finns fired at them from the shelter of rocks and trees, and one boat 'hit a little stone' and stuck fast. The others retreated but the stranded boat took several casualties before its commander very sensibly surrendered.

We found a monument on the shore commemorating this victory over the British at the 'battle of Halkokari', but there was yet more to see. In a park near Kokkola there was a glass-fronted building containing the actual boat captured on that occasion, a beautifully built vessel with double skin diagonal planking.

The comparatively easy rule of the Czar continued for some time. We saw traces of this at its most benign on the island of Högsåra. It seems that Czar Alexander III, who died in 1894, developed a taste for yachting and cruised the islands with his wife. On Högsåra there was a small hut, unlocked and accessible to all, which served as a museum of the Czar's visits and highlighted the friendship that had grown up between him and a local fisher-woman. The place in consequence was called Kejsarhamn. Even the charts we had used to get there had their origin in the Russian era, which is why their appearance is so different from that of their Swedish counterparts.

Ironically it was the first stirrings of democracy in Russia that made the Finns turn their minds to independence. Whereas the Czars had kept Finland autonomous the Russian Assembly, flexing its muscles, insisted that it should be an integral part of Russia. The Revolution of 1917 restored autonomy but by then the issue of independence was in the air. Lenin appears to have accepted the Finnish position, perhaps in anticipation of a Communist takeover, but in any case he had wider issues on his mind at the time. What had not been foreseen was a ferocious civil war in Finland, which led in 1918 to a victory of the White Guards, with some German help, over the Red Guards. General Mannerheim, the architect of victory, led his troops into Helsinki and Finland was established as a sovereign state.

Thus it was, when years later we sailed into Kemi in the far north we found there were two yacht clubs, one socialist and one conservative. Reminders of such divisions among the Finnish people met us wherever we went. In more southerly ports there were also two clubs, but there one would be Swedish speaking and the other Finnish. And there was evidence in the attitude of people we met that these estrangements have yet to be consigned to history, once and for all time.

All this contrasts strongly with the comparatively monolithic nature of the Swedish population. Naturally there are differences between Swedes living on the west coast and those on the east, between the people of Stockholm and those of the countryside, and most noticeably to us, between the somewhat rigid south and the more free and easy north. Such differences occur, or are thought to occur, in most nations. They are normally far less significant than differences between the individuals you meet. The divisions in

Finland run deeper. To see how, in spite of these, the Finns came to weld together an effective nation required a stroll through the churchyard on the island of Nauvo.

Here were the gravestones of the dead of the Winter War fought in 1939 and 1940. The war had its origins in Russian anxiety over the closeness of the border with Finland to the great city of Leningrad. Seeing the growth of Hitler's military power the Soviet Union demanded a change to the line of the frontier and the right to establish bases in Finnish territory. The Finns refused so the Red Army attacked in strength. Western nations could do little to help and Finland fought alone until beaten. Casualties were high and deeds of heroism innumerable.

And there in Nauvo were the graves of those from the island who had fallen, Swedish speaking and Finnish speaking alike. The Finnish army had been so organised that people from the same community fought together. While this undoubtedly improved morale and teamwork it also meant that in a disaster the young men of a village would all die together. The cost of the war was plain to see, but so was the pride in the resistance that had been mounted against vastly superior forces. As Pertti Korttila, a native Finnish speaker who was fluent in Swedish and in English, put it: 'Well, I know we didn't exactly win that war, but we came a bloody good second!'

Unhappily the Winter War was not the end of the affair. In the same churchyard we found to our surprise just as many headstones as were dedicated to the Winter War with dates on them between 1943 and 1944. These were the graves of the victims of what is known as the Continuation War. When Hitler invaded Russia the Finns unwisely became involved on the German side. This was not enormously destructive to either of the combatants at first, but once the German armies were in retreat the Russians attacked their Finnish allies in overwhelming force. The Finns called once again on their old hero, now Field Marshal Mannerheim, to negotiate the best terms he could get.

These involved leasing parts of the Finnish archipelago to the

Soviet Union, which were duly returned when the lease came to an end in 1956. The Finns also kept their side of the bargain. Finland never became a satellite Communist state, but was bound closely to Russia by economic ties and adopted a strictly neutral stance in the Cold War.

In the end this worked out very well for the Finns. With a guaranteed market for half her exports, mainly timber, Finland was free to develop new industries such as electronics and shipbuilding, which opened up markets in the west. So that when the Cold War came to an end, she was ready to stake her claim to a full place in the new Europe.

Just how far and how fast Finland has moved over the last century was revealed to us by a monument we found in Hanko, on the outskirts of the elegant Old Town. It depicted flying swans, symbolising the emigration which took place through this port in the late nineteenth and early twentieth centuries. While the rich here enjoyed their ornate villas by the sea, life for many Finns was hard enough to prompt them to seek a life overseas. Beginning in 1883, when a steamer route from Hanko to Hull was opened, over 300,000 passed through on their way to countries offering an escape from *'foeda paupertas'*. A census taken in the USA in 1910 showed that by then 200,000 Finns had already arrived there.

In the flesh, or feather, Finnish swans are very similar to our own. Yet Finns see them in an altogether different light. Their swans are not creatures of river or pond, gratefully accepting crusts of bread thrown to them by children. Theirs are wild birds flying out into the unknown in pursuit of one last, elusive hope. These are the swans to be seen on the monument at Hanko, or heard in the music of Sibelius, or perhaps even more so in the 'Cantus Arcticus' of Rautavaara.

After all this it is perhaps not surprising that as we sailed between Finland and Sweden, meeting and mingling with people in either country, we seemed to find some broad differences that may, or may not, have been related to the course of history. Was it our imagination or were the Finns less romantic and more reckless than their friends across the water? But that cannot be so: the people of the north are all romantic, and especially the sailors amongst them. It may be just that romanticism has two aspects, love and adventure, and that Finns have been accustomed to living dangerously for the last hundred years or so.

When we turned towards the southern shore of the Baltic we were no longer looking back at history, but witnessing it in the making. For many years that coast had been a no-go area for yachtsmen, once past the borders of West Germany. There had been a gradual thaw, enough to enable us to visit Poland in 1988, when the Communists were in power. But even then the harbour office was guarded by a soldier with a machine gun. East Germany was off-limits entirely. Awful warnings were issued to sailors about the consequences of wandering into East German waters, and in particular of entering any of the military areas which projected from the coastline.

By 1991 all this had changed. The Iron Curtain had dissolved and both Poland and East Germany were in the process of adjusting to a change of regime and to a different way of life. It seemed an ideal time to make a visit.

We sailed across from Klintholm in Denmark, intending to put in to Stralsund, but storms and strong winds made Saßnitz, on the eastern side of Rügen, a safer landfall. The harbour at Saßnitz was very full and quite uncomfortable. There had, after all, been no time as yet to make provision for visiting yachts. The town itself was dilapidated, buildings and streets alike looking as if no work had been done on them for years. But walls now sprouted satellite television aerials, there were eager queues in video shops, and attempts were being made to cater for visitors, even if these consisted of little more than beer tents.

We waited for a day for the wind to subside, then set off for Poland. It was still blowing force 5 or 6 from the west, so 'Sea Bear' stopped outside the harbour while I put a reef in her mainsail. After that, with the wind on her starboard quarter, she took off like a rocket, leaving behind some larger German yachts that had been compelled to reef more deeply. Along with them we found a sheltered place in Swinoujscie harbour. This town too seemed run-down, and one of the reasons for that was plain to see at the far end of the quay.

There, moored alongside each other, were a dozen or more gun-boats. They had patrolled the River Oder on the Polish side of the border with East Germany, matched boat for boat by the Germans. There is no doubt that this had been in the recent past one of Europe's more sensitive frontiers. At the end of the 1939-1945 war it had seen millions of Germans expelled by the Poles in retaliation for all the miseries inflicted on them by the Nazis. I had however been mistaken in believing that this had marked the end of hostil-ities. For within what people in the west had been inclined to see as a seamless Communist empire, there had in fact been a great deal of tension. Here, along the line of the Oder there had been a Cold War within the Cold War, and one that, considering the strength of the armaments deployed, might well have led to shooting – certainly no place for a yacht to have ventured.

A few days later, in passing Peenemünde, we looked into the harbour to see another forest of gunboat masts, about the same number as we had found in Swinoujscie, only of course German this time. The sight of two such metal graveyards was surely a cause for rejoicing, of welcoming a return to sanity in a part of the world that seemed to have abandoned it. Yet a sneaky feeling lurked at the edges of my mind that those still sinister ships, so carefully main-tained, had a greater hope of resurrection than the dead of Nauvo or of Arnis.

At Peenemünde thoughts of this nature were perhaps inspired by the great black sheds which loomed over the bright green marshes like some weird construction from an alien world. Here was the place where in the last war Hitler's V1 flying bombs and V2 rockets had been produced: which evoked memories of my youth, when the sound of a V1 engine cutting out before the inevitable explosion, or the double crack of a rocket arriving unannounced from the stratosphere were daily events.

If reflections of this nature crossed our minds, it was for a moment only. We were after all in 1991, the reeds were indeed green, and all around Rügen there was hope of a better future. The passing of a darker era was marked in Ueckermünde by a sign on the wall of the village square. It said simply 'Markt', while below was an older sign with the former title 'Karl Marx Platz', meticulously maintained, but with a diagonal line across it.

And hope imbued the little harbour at Stralsund. The harbourmaster there explained some of the difficulties that yachtsmen had faced under the previous regime. The aspect which earned my deepest respect was that yachting had continued there at all. True, the boats were small and fitted out with much home-made equipment, but the enthusiasm was tangible.

Possibly our fondest memory of that spring-like summer was of a visit to the Polish National Sailing School at Trzebiez, because it was here that we felt ourselves to be in a very small way participants in, rather than just observers of, the changes taking place. We sailed into the harbour to make fast to a buoy astern, with our bow right under the School's tall flagstaff. Strict flag etiquette was observed morning and evening, although the morning parade, when orders for the day were read, seemed fairly informal, not least because it was attended by cadets of either sex, and one small dog.

Now we were pretty confident of our flag drill and had taken care to come equipped with the proper courtesy ensign. Poland, like Great Britain, has a marine flag that differs from the national flag used ashore. Instead of plain white and red the Polish marine flag has a shield in the white half, with an eagle on it. This we hoisted proudly, with perhaps a sideways glance at some visiting German yachts which appeared not to have appreciated the difference.

To my chagrin I was informed in the harbour office that our flag was incorrect. There had been a recent change and the eagle now had to wear a crown. In fact it had worn a crown in years past, but the Communists had removed it. Now, with the end of Communism, the crown was being reinstated. 'What sort of a crown?'

I asked. And armed with the appropriate diagram I returned to 'Sea Bear' where Joy embroidered a crown for our eagle.

So at eight the following morning up went our newly-crowned eagle and honour was restored. That day we had in fact made history, since even the Sailing School's own flag had yet to have its eagle crowned. Somehow I doubt that the hoisting of the first correct flag at Trzebiez will be recorded in any history book, but I do recall that the people there were exceptionally kind to us during the remainder of our stay.

We left the southern shore of the Baltic from Darßer Ort, then a small East German harbour with a rotting landing stage, a place which had been, until quite recently, a naval base. The ornate gates remained but the area had been turned into a camping site, with a little yellow train to take children for a ride. It seemed a fitting point of departure. We put out to sea on a bright, sunny morning to disappear almost immediately into a thick bank of fog, from which we did not emerge until we reached Gedser in Denmark and found the sun again. The experience of moving through that uniform greyness had a strange quality about it, as if we were passing from one world to another.

CHAPTER FIVE

Into the Dark

Huuman beings are creatures of the day. Much of life may have to be spent in darkness, but that seems to me a deplorable fact rather than a cause for celebration. It is however a fact which has to be taken into consideration by those who wish to cross the North Sea in boats capable of averaging not much more than five knots.

In our early years of sailing I met a number of yacht club hearties keen to make a virtue of necessity. Almost any passage was better made at night. 'Much better, old boy, less crowded, and you can spot the lighthouses from a far greater distance.' They may, I suspect, have been lucky, but even then I saw the night as colder, damper and altogether more dangerous. Very little has happened since to change my mind. After all, to spot lighthouses you need a clear sky, not a murky one sitting heavily on a sea full of large ships going about their business with scant regard for small yachts, while you are at the helm fighting a natural urge to sleep.

Of course there were compensations. Our memories of night sailing range from flat calms to gales, from bright moonlight to blinding rain or fog, and include some of the most exhilarating voyages we have made. Then there is that wonderful feeling of relaxation when, in harbour again and securely moored, you stretch out on your bunk for sleep of a quality few landsmen could ever experience.

At this juncture I propose to leave the few stormy nights we encountered until later, where they form part of a wider look at heavy weather, and concentrate on what night sailing in general meant for Joy and for me. Over the years we settled into a routine which suited us, but might have had little relevance for larger, stronger crews. For the most part there would be just the two of us, sometimes with one or other, or with both of our children.

Under these circumstances we found it advisable to go into the night rested and fully prepared. This favoured a morning start with a day ahead of us before meeting darkness far from land. That gave time to make all preparations in a leisurely way. As evening came on we would each try to rest for an hour or two, and to enjoy a hot meal while daylight remained. The passage plan for the night would have been worked out in advance, with a note of the direction of tidal streams and the likely times at which we should be able to sight any useful buoys or lighthouses. I would also have taken down the latest weather forecast received, although this may have been some time before.

As the light began to fade I would look around the horizon to try to get a feel for the weather to come, over and above the official predictions. It was not of course always reliable, any more than the forecasts received by radio were totally reliable, but it did have a bearing on one decision that had to be made there and then, whether or not to reef for the night ahead.

We had deck lights to help if I had to go forward to reef in the dark and used them from time to time. But moving about the deck in full oilskins while trailing a line from my safety harness was at best a clumsy business. The chances that something would snag somewhere were fewer in daylight, so it was often the case that I would take in a precautionary reef while there was still light enough to see what I was doing.

In 'Bugle' and in 'Bunting' there was one further task on deck, to hoist our bulky radar reflector up into the rigging. This was the size of a small dustbin and was supposed to make us visible to large ships long before they could spot our navigation lights. It hung beneath the crosstrees and clattered about in the rigging all night long. By the time we had 'Sea Bear' we had had more than enough of that, so she was equipped with a smaller reflector fixed permanently to the mast in a higher position.

Whether either of these devices really worked we shall never know. Certainly they made us feel safer, and no large ship ever did run us down, so maybe they did.

After these preparations it remained to decide on the pattern of our night watches. Watch keeping with a larger crew can be quite rigid, so that everyone gets a period of rest at fixed intervals. If more than one night is to be spent at sea this is highly desirable, and we observed it, for example, crossing from Norway to Scotland with Tom. But normally there was little chance of a second night since we planned to make harbour by early afternoon at the latest, and usually the crew was just the two of us. So we treated it all quite informally, deciding on the spot who would take the first watch and so on, according to how each of us felt at the time. One or the other of us might well feel more alert as darkness came on, and happier to continue until the other had had some sleep.

The watch we both preferred was the one which saw the dawn break. There was nothing quite like seeing the sun come up out of the sea on those precious occasions when a clear sky allowed it. Even on bad, grey days everything tended to look less threatening and more manageable as the light returned. In arranging our time-tables we tried to share these dawn watches fairly.

This was made easier by a certain flexibility in the time we each spent in the cockpit. Generally two hours was enough, but on warmer, drier nights this might be extended. In emergencies, of course the only limit was your physical and mental ability to stay at the helm.

When all these preparations had been made whoever was to take the first watch would put on as many pullovers as required, clamber into oilskins and safety harness, take hold of woolly hat and gloves and settle in the cockpit. Around the watch keeper's neck was hung a small compass, so that if a ship was sighted bearings could be taken to ensure that we were not on a collision course.

In our earlier years watch keeping meant helming for most of the time. The first generation of automatic steering devices seemed to work only in ideal conditions. By the time we had 'Sea Bear' they had become much more powerful, and 'Sea Bear' was so beautifully balanced under almost any conditions that only minor adjustments were required from time to time. So watch keeping came to mean checking that we remained on course, adjusting the sails to cope with any wind shift and, above all, keeping a good look-out.

This last was not as easy as it might seem. The spray hood gave protection but obstructed some of the view forward. Seats were on either side of the cockpit so that from any one position you could never observe the whole horizon; there was always a blind spot at the back of your head. Shifting from side to side and occasionally standing to peer over the spray hood helped, and also served to keep you awake.

Other aids to wakefulness and comfort during night watches were slabs of home-made fruit cake and at some stage a mug of 'North Sea coffee'. This was no more than instant coffee to which a good measure of cognac had been added. It is strange how family names persist. Even in the tideless waters of the Gulf of Bothnia we still had North Sea coffee to warm us at night.

All the preparations we made for night sailing were quite practical, resembling the cockpit drills of an airline pilot before take off, or the weapon checks a soldier makes when going into battle. Yet there was an element of ritual about them, as if correct observance could, in some magical way, ward off the perils of the dark. I suspect that this psychological aspect was at least as important as reefing or radar reflectors, for it meant that, once the ritual was complete, we were mentally prepared for a night at sea.

This is why we planned our later voyages to allow all such tasks to be done at a leisurely pace, placing the night sail in the centre, with plenty of daylight on either side. In our earlier years we had too often attempted to start and finish a long passage in the course of a day, only to find that sunset came exactly as predicted and there was nothing we could do to postpone it. So if things had not gone according to plan we would find ourselves tired and frustrated at the moment when we had to face the additional challenge of entering a strange harbour in the dark.

A number of uncomfortable memories cluster around situations of this kind. One that might stand for all of them is the recollection of a botched approach to the German island of Helgoland, which I made in the course of the family's long voyage to Oxelösund in 'Bunting'. To make the best of the tidal stream we had delayed our start from Norderney, so that time was in any case all too short. Then, failing to get a good RDF signal to check our position, I let the tide carry us right past the island, so that as evening drew on and Helgoland's great lighthouse came alive, I was faced with motoring up to the harbour against both the current and a stiffening breeze.

It was wet work, and to make things worse the way in was marked by unlit buoys, not huge but large enough to do damage should we hit one in the dark. There were however leading lights to guide us in. Normally these gave me no trouble. All I had to do was to keep them in line until I was safely in harbour. Here the critical part of the approach relied on a single light of a type I dreaded. This was a sectored beam which showed white while you were on course, and turned red or green if you strayed to either side. In such a narrow channel these colour changes could follow each other quite rapidly, and I had great difficulty in recognising them.

My colour blindness was far from complete and seldom caused problems. Large ships or fishing boats were plain enough to see and it was not difficult to determine their direction. My job was to ensure that they did not get close enough for their red or green lights to matter. But if they did, at least there were two separate and distinct lights, one red, one green, not a light which kept changing colour. So I rarely had to call on my crew for help, although I made sure that I always sailed with someone who had perfect sight. Since colour blindness does not seem to affect women as much as men, Joy became colour consultant as well as first mate, and had the final word in any argument about a given light.

In the approach to Helgoland there was no time for arguments.

We went in with me at the helm and a daughter on either side calling, 'Dad, it's turning green,' or 'OK Dad, it's white again' until we were safely within the harbour walls. It was by then long past their bedtime and they did not seem to enjoy peering out of the cockpit into the flying spray at a time when we had all hoped to be snugly in our bunks. Perhaps the recognition that their skipper could, and occasionally did, make mistakes increased their anxiety level. It had after all been as good an example of how not to plan and execute a voyage as anyone could have wished.

Unplanned and unwelcome excursions into the dark were few after Helgoland, but they did occur, and were not always the fault of the skipper. Some twelve years later we were involved in one which was quite unexpected and potentially far more dangerous.

'Sea Bear' was at Hals on the east coast of Jutland. She was on passage to Norway, where Joy's sister was to meet us for a gentle ascent by canal into the mountains of Telemark. Weather forecasts for the day ahead were somewhat evasive, although there was a hint of south westerly winds to come. We left Hals quite early in a flat calm and motored northward with the intention of deciding later whether to put into another Danish harbour or to cross the Skaggerak by night to make our landfall in Norway the next morning. By mid-afternoon the warm, hazy weather seemed set to continue for some hours at least so we checked our fuel supplies and decided to head for Langesund in Norway.

Early evening saw us clear of the Skaw, that long, curved point of flat land protruding from the tip of Jutland. Now we had to cross the shipping lanes. Commercial shipping entering the Skaggerak from the North Sea always takes the shortest route it can so the waters around the point of the Skaw were busy with large vessels moving in either direction. 'Sea Bear' was nicely between the stream of ships going eastward and those heading out of the Skaggerak when, at 18.40, she came to a sudden halt.

Looking over the side we could see a huge sheet of thick, black plastic. Later we were able to read the dimensions printed on it: 100

metres by 50 metres. It seems to have been some sort of hatch cover and, from the wording on it, appeared to have come from a Dutch cargo vessel. Whether it was still complete or not we shall never know. What was clear was that it was wrapped around our propeller and also around the rudder.

'Sea Bear' was fitted with cutters ahead of the propeller to deal with debris of one kind or another. These worked well enough on stray ropes but were helpless against so large and flexible an enemy as this. Now we had a real problem, made worse by the fact that the rudder was also affected.

A few years earlier we had experienced a similar incident in the Gulf of Gdansk. There Joy had volunteered to go over the side with a knife to free the propeller. She could swim, but I tied a rope around her as a safety precaution. After a struggle in the murky water she emerged with a large sheet of plastic, apparently blown off a building site, which we carried triumphantly back to Sweden.

This time I rejected Joy's offer to go over the side. It was far too dangerous, for the whole area around the stern was seething with black plastic. Instead I pulled as much of it as I could into the cockpit, where it lay in a damp and sullen heap, but there was clearly much more still in the water.

So there we sat, becalmed with large ships passing close by on either side. It has to be admitted that if we had had VHF radio I would have used it to request a tow out of this predicament, for as the sun began to set the prospect of spending a night with only our feeble navigation lights and a small radar reflector to show passing traffic that we were there did not appeal. In retrospect this was the only time I regretted the lack of VHF, but fortunately that regret did not last long.

By 22.00 a light wind had sprung up from the south and we were able to set full sail and beat slowly against it down the coast towards Skagen. Because of the plastic around the rudder turns to port were difficult, and we were trailing so much of it that we could barely manage four knots even in a steadily rising wind. Navigation had to be precise because the chart showed rows of posts to which fishing nets were attached extending some way from the coast in this area. Our clumsy turns had to be made in good time before these unseen hazards were encountered.

In this fashion we eventually reached the fishing port of Skagen, and after our usual arguments about red and green lights, which were not easy to distinguish among all the other lights on the shore, we tacked for the entrance. A fishing boat was leaving at the time, heading straight for us until the skipper noticed our lights. He could hardly have expected to meet a yacht sailing very slowly with limited manoeuvring power at that time of night. In normal circumstances no sensible yacht would attempt to enter Skagen under sail.

The harbour was large with several basins, one of which offered a restricted mooring space for yachts. We had to tack between high walls from one basin to another until we spotted a few pleasure craft and made our way towards them. The wind of course came off the walls in more than one direction. I found it helped to think of myself as a Broads sailor once more, used to handling boats under sail in narrow places and in fluky winds. And 'Sea Bear' hampered as she was, became for a few minutes a genuine Broads yacht, slipping between those high and hard-looking walls with no trouble at all.

Joy went forward to lower the mainsail on my signal while I attempted to come alongside a German yacht without waking her crew: it was by then 02.00. Needless to say I failed. We stopped neatly enough but inevitably had to step on our neighbour's deck to make fast. This roused an indignant skipper in his underwear, whose attitude changed the moment he saw our sails hastily dropped to the deck and a large pile of black plastic in the cockpit.

By the time a diver had completed his work the next day there was an even larger pile of plastic on the quayside. No damage appeared to have been done, so after a day of rest we set out at 04.15 on the following morning to meet the rising sun and enjoy an uneventful crossing to Norway.

Once we had established our routine for night sailing we seldom experienced emergencies on the scale of Skagen. Even in our earlier years things could occasionally go as planned. Our first night at sea as a family seemed to corroborate the views of those stalwarts of the yacht club who had trumpeted the virtues of the dark.

We had taken 'Bugle' down to the West Country and were returning along the French coast. Our stay at Fécamp had been pleasant enough, but was prolonged to the point of frustration by a westerly gale which piled up a heavy sea outside the harbour and sent an uncomfortable surge in amongst the moorings. Only one yacht had tried to leave and that had been dashed against the piers and damaged. Eventually there came a day when the wind moderated to just a stiff breeze, so we left at around noon with the possibility of putting into Dieppe or of sailing through the night to Boulogne.

With a fair wind and a sea that became less rough with every hour we made good time and reached Dieppe with plenty of daylight to spare. A family consultation then took place to decide whether to enter the harbour or to sail on. If we continued on our way we would naturally have to contend with an adverse tidal stream which can run quite strongly near the French coast. But 'Bugle' was romping along at a speed that would make light work of any foul tide. The sea might get rougher when our favourable wind came up against the tidal stream, but it should still be less lumpy than it had been on leaving Fécamp. How did everyone feel?

All the family were in favour of continuing. After some days in port the idea of wasting the wind we then had did not appeal, so I had no need to use my casting vote as skipper. We went about making our preparations for the night ahead. Watch keeping was of course to be primarily up to Joy and me, but both Katy and Helen took the opportunity to stand a watch along with one or other of us, and to helm the boat as she charged through the night.

The sky was clear and starry, the weather comparatively warm and the brilliant French lighthouses could be seen for miles out at sea. This meant that bearings could be taken on the one you were leaving behind and on the next one ahead, so that the yacht's position could be fixed with accuracy at almost any point. It felt as if we were being passed along the coast from one friendly lighthouse to the next.

Dawn saw us approaching Boulogne, so another decision had to be made. It would not be easy to find a berth that early in the day, before any of the craft that had stayed overnight had moved, while we had all the daylight we could wish for to reach Ramsgate, and the wind was still with us. We turned to cross the shipping lanes and headed for home.

We arrived at mid-day, with the intention of buying essential supplies while the shops were still open. However Joy and I felt that first we needed a little sleep and stretched out on our bunks for half an hour. When we woke evening was coming on and there was no time left for shopping, but to our delight the children had found some money, made their way into the town, and bought all that was required. The least we could do was to take them out for a fish and chip supper, to celebrate our return to England.

As time went on Joy and I had to manage nights at sea mainly on our own, although on one occasion we picked up some passengers on the way. This was eleven years later, when 'Sea Bear' set out on the journey north that took her eventually into the Gulf of Bothnia. By that time we had grown more ambitious in the distances we would expect to cover in a day and a night, and more confident of our boat's ability to handle whatever weather we might meet.

Our destination was Texel, the first of the Dutch Frisian Islands. Once out of Harwich Harbour we enjoyed a south-easterly breeze which increased in strength throughout the day, until we were travelling at a good six knots or more. As evening came on I took in a reef in preparation for the night, but this did not seem to affect our speed unduly. Throughout all the hours of darkness 'Sea Bear' ploughed on, with occasional changes of course to correct the leeway we were making, which was drifting us too far to the north.

At first light our visitors arrived. These were racing pigeons whose navigation had gone awry. They had become exhausted flying in so brisk a wind. One had already fallen into the sea when it noticed our arrival, managed somehow to take to the air again and scrambled aboard. Two others followed, so now we had one roosting in the bunt of the sail formed by the reef I had taken, and two in the cockpit, hooking their feet into the coils of my foresail sheets to keep a precarious balance on a deck that was moving quite sharply under them.

This was the first time we had appreciated that birds could get seasick. The mess in the cockpit was considerable, and impossible to clear away while the birds kept a grim hold of my ropes. Then we were hit by a heavy squall and drenching rain. I got soaked dealing with the sails, while the pigeons decided they would be better off in the cabin. By the time I came back to the cockpit two of them were perched on a rail overlooking the chart table, for all the world as if they were checking our course and destination.

Naturally that could not be allowed. A mess in the cockpit was bad enough, but my chart table was a hallowed spot, sacred to the gods of navigation. One by one I picked them up, explained that they were deck cargo, not cabin passengers, and set them outside, back on their coils of rope. We tried to feed them water and breadcrumbs, but they were not that hungry.

By this time I had made the decision to abandon Texel, use the northerly drift which had carried us a little too far for a comfortable approach to the Schulpengat, and carry on for the island of Vlieland. As we drew closer to our destination two of the birds flew off towards the island. The third got tangled with the mainsheet as we gybed at the entrance buoy and broke its neck. We buried it at sea on the way in, a sad heap of soft, grey-green feathers, soon lost to sight astern.

That cast a small shadow on what had been one of our finest and fastest night passages. There was an exceptional amount of cleaning to do in the cockpit after we had arrived in port, but two of the birds had found safety, and for all I knew, companionship, since the woods on Vlieland resounded with the cooing of pigeons.

Visitors of a more threatening kind attended our last night at sea. We were returning from our belated foray into the Bay of

Biscay, conscious that as a crew we now lacked the physical strength that had served us in the past. To augment our frailty Joy had fallen in Morgat and hurt her leg. A visit to the hospital showed no broken bones, but the leg remained very tender and the least movement on the boat caused her pain.

As a result I picked our weather carefully and reached St.Peter Port on Guernsey mainly by motoring through flat calms. From there I had planned to go to Cherbourg before crossing the Channel, but received a weather report which changed my mind. A high pressure system had settled overhead and was likely to stay for a day or two. The forecast was for light winds and good visibility. If we were ever to avoid too much movement in 'Sea Bear', now was the time to sail. So the plan was redrawn to encompass a voyage direct from Guernsey to the Solent, avoiding if at all possible the worst of the overfalls in the Alderney Race.

The passage through the Little Russel channel and the Race itself was fast and at times lumpy, even with no discernible wind. The tide hurried us on at such a pace that in the course of an evening we cleared all the various hazards of that alarming patch of sea, and were then free to relax and set a course across the Channel. As it grew dark the moon came up behind us to throw a beam of light across the water, pointing the way home. For a while I believed we were in for one of those rare, magical nights when you would not wish to be anywhere else but at sea.

Soon after midnight I changed my mind. The bright moonbeam astern of us was invaded by the dark silhouette of a vessel which looked remarkably like a gunboat. It closed at speed and then shone a searchlight on to us. There was nothing I could do about that, so I simply maintained course and hoped that whoever was in charge would be satisfied with what he had seen. The stranger then dropped behind again, but lowered a dinghy into which dark shapes embarked, five or six of them. It was clear we were to have visitors.

They boarded 'Sea Bear' with ease and announced themselves as French Customs. The leader was a young lady, petite but with a large pistol on her hip. Now in the past we had had several encounters with armed officialdom and knew the rules. First it is necessary to remember that they are not foreigners, you are. Then it is certain that bluster will achieve nothing, but make matters rapidly worse. Finally it is dangerous to assume that any official has a sense of humour. So we answered all their questions, produced our own and the ship's papers and said goodbye to them half an hour later.

Now the character of our night at sea had been changed. At first I had assigned it to that rare class of 'romantic' nights, to be included with memories of the bright moon that had seen us all the way from Norway to Scotland, or of that marvellous illuminated sky in the Gulf of Bothnia, just as Tacitus had described it, nearly two thousand years before. The thought remained, but had been overlaid by images of gunboats and recollections of being stopped and questioned, or led into port for a more detailed examination. This particular episode was hardly an extreme instance and served more to confuse than to redefine.

It had been a sense of occasion, the knowledge that this would be our last night at sea together, and a seductive moon that had lured me into a false sentimentality. Memories cannot be ordered in advance or wilfully invested with this or that character. And on reflection the very notion of a romantic night is open to question. There are too many anxieties at sea for that.

It may indeed be a mistake to classify some nights as more romantic than others, or even to use that overworked and trivialised word. The truth is something deeper. For, whatever the weather, man and wife are never closer than when one is resting, chocked between the lee bunk and the side of the ship as she heels, listening to the burble of the water against the hull, while the other is outside in the cockpit, muffled against the cold, keeping watch over the sea and over everything that is held dear. Those who have not experienced this may have something yet to learn about marriage.

All this means that it would be hard to nominate a typical night at sea. There are so many different memories from which to choose. But if I give my mind free rein what comes to the fore is not gales or bright lighthouses or moonbeams, or even Tacitean sunsets and sunrises. It is a night of mist and damp, when drops of water fall from the boom on to your head and your woolly gloves are covered with beads of moisture. The distance you can see is uncertain. There is no horizon and the mist reflects your navigation lamps, so that you appear to be travelling in a globe of light.

Then out of the darkness and on to the edge of your vision floats a fulmar, silently with hardly a movement of its wings, showing white against the glowing mist. At dawn the bird vanishes. You seldom see its going. It is just that when individual waves can be seen clearly and the horizon opens out, there is no bird there.

The relationship you have with the fulmar is not close. This is a wild, ocean bird, not a pigeon to be held in your hands and cared for as best you may. But birds need vision and hate mist and fog. Your boat, moving slowly as it does, gives the fulmar a fixed point around which it can fly. For you, as the bird moves in and out of the circle of light it brings a sense of comfort, assurance that you are here on earth, at sea, and not somewhere out in a grey nothingness between worlds.

CHAPTER SIX

The Influence of Birds and Beasts

B IRDS MATTER TO SAILORS. They form a link between land and water, making the sea less of a lonely place to be. They are also important in defining where you are, the nature of that portion of the globe to which you have sailed. Rather as a knowledge of history adds depth to your perception of a land and its inhabitants, so the sight and sound of birds overlays an impression of cliffs and creeks, of harbours and the countryside surrounding them, to provide an extra dimension, which in this case is not the product of thought but of sensation, felt immediately and etched on the memory of places visited.

Beasts have a role in this also, but because birds have the freedom of the air and less need to hide they inevitably play the major part. These creatures impinge directly on the eyes and ears, but there is often something else to be observed and that is the attitude of people to the birds and beasts around them. That too can be important in understanding what it might be like to live in, say, Schleswig-Holstein or in the far north of Sweden.

Now Joy and I are by no means naturalists or bird-watchers. We did not go to sea armed with telescopes, tripods or little notebooks to mark down this or that species. Nor did we seek out nature reserves or places where birds and animals are carefully protected from mankind. The creatures we met were simply there, part of the total experience of being wherever we were. They seemed to me to be one vital element in a picture which included, rather than excluded, humans.

We are now living in Manningtree, at the head of navigation of the River Stour, which enters the sea a few miles to the east at Harwich. The town is attractive in its own right, with streets leading upwards from the river, old houses, good pubs and a small, but well-attended, market. In summer it even entertains the odd tourist.

What makes it special for us, and gives it a character all its own, is the geese. They fly low over the houses, calling to each other continually. There are often just four or five of them, flying in a ragged V. But at the peak times for migrants they come in their hundreds, in wide formations of which parts only can be glimpsed between the roofs and chimney pots. The sky is then filled with their incessant chatter. What are they saying to each other? To our anthropomorphic ears they sound cheerful, but it may be just our hearts that are lifted by the sight and sound of them. Without the geese in our skyscape Manningtree would be a duller place.

So it was too with the Broadland birds that enriched our earlier years together. Now they have become an advertising cliché. Boat hirers beckon you with visions of quiet, bird-haunted waters. The reality is a little different. In summer time the bird calls are lost in the noise of engines as a steady procession of hire craft moves up and down those narrow rivers. Yet the birds are still there and do not seem to mind. At dusk when the motor boats have fallen silent they can be seen going about their business as they have always done.

The heron still stands sentinel on a reach he has claimed as his own; the grebe still dodges in and out of the reedbeds. That grebe could well be the first one that I ever saw, unaged, immune to the passing of years. As I sail past in the failing light it seems that nothing has changed. The birds were there before us and will be there when the motor boats are long gone. The character of the Broads is defined by them, not by us. Yet it is not completely immutable, or I would see once again the wake of a coypu, swimming across the river as the mist gathers over the water.

The transition from our life on the Broads to sailing on the open sea was marked by a drastic change in the nature of the birds we met. They became wilder, more carnivorous and generally louder. Nothing could typify the change more dramatically than the sight of gannets fishing off the coast of Scotland. These huge birds flew high over the water then quite suddenly trimmed their great wings and plunged straight downwards beneath the waves. The sight of twenty or thirty of them together, splashing into the sea at random intervals, with the spray from their impact gleaming in the sunshine is hard to forget.

It is not of course peculiar to Scotland because gannets are wide ranging ocean birds, but in memory they have become associated with the Western Isles, along with more restrained puffins and guillemots.

In the course of our travels it did seem that certain birds would become linked with very specific areas, however far they might in fact roam. This does not mean that they came to symbolise any given place for us. Our memories were too direct and too complex for that. But the birds often formed one layer of a composite recollection of places, people and events.

As an example, consider how recollections of the Frisian Islands are underpinned by residual images garnered from 'The Riddle of the Sands'. These are then confirmed by first hand impressions of sandbanks, mud and low-lying islands, of the wind in my face and the sight of steep seas in the *Seegat*. But what makes the experience something more than just an echo of Erskine Childers, and something which is very clearly mine, is the sound of oyster catchers. Their continuous piping rises and falls, then reaches a crescendo which arches over the water and the sands to add a further dimension to what was already a multi-layered experience. And once added it cannot be taken away. Those birds will always be part of the Frisian Islands.

Thus it was that as we passed through the canal into the Baltic and north into the Gulf of Bothnia other birds took over, to help define the memory of what we found there. It seemed to me that once we had entered the Gulf birds lost their appetite for song. Of course they still made a noise but it was not the glorious sound you hear when blackbirds and thrushes lead the chorus at home. There the thrush appeared to have been replaced by a near relative, the fieldfare. In Swedish the bird was called *björktrast* or 'birch thrush', but the noise it made could hardly be called a song. Instead it produced a squawk which became most agitated when it defended its eggs from marauding magpies.

Even the smaller birds seemed less interested in music. There was a large population of pied wagtails, cheerful enough and seemingly unafraid of humans, but relatively quiet. I recall sitting in a coffee shop in Ulvöhamn watching a pair of wagtails teaching their huge chick to fly. They had every incentive to succeed, because keeping him supplied with food must have proved exhausting. He was of course a cuckoo. It seems that cuckoos frequently choose wagtails to rear their young. Perhaps they have a reputation for conscientious parenting.

Before we set out on our travels we had no idea of how far north cuckoos would fly in summer. We had our first inkling of this at Gieslau, just off the Nord-Ostsee canal. There we looked out over the marshes to see a pair of them flying together, something neither of us had seen before. Even that did not prepare us for the sound of cuckoos calling in the northern archipelago, just as loudly as they had on the River Orwell, over a thousand miles away. There was however no chance of the cuckoo becoming our bird of the north, possibly because in those parts he felt to us like a brazen intruder, or maybe because we had already claimed him for our home river and given him residential status in Woolverstone and Pin Mill.

Neither could fieldfares, magpies or wagtails qualify. They were fun and part of our memory of the north, but not a defining part. The bird that came closest to that was the eider. Naturally we saw more of them than we did of other birds because we spent more time on the water. For the same reason we also saw them near-at-hand, since they seemed to take visiting yachts for granted. Their soft, sighing voices could often be heard right alongside as we lay at anchor.

We anchored once in a completely sheltered lagoon known locally as 'Paradise Basin'. It lies in the heart of the Stockholm archipelago and is one of the comparatively few places protected from all winds. We went there to ride out a severe gale that was forecast to last a couple of days.

Over to starboard a rock projected from the water and on it an eider stood guard over her dead chick. Another bird swam some distance away, calling from time to time, coaxing her to leave what could not be saved and rejoin the flock. At first I thought it was her mate, but that could never have been the case. Male eiders take no part in caring for their young, and in fact there were no males in Paradise Basin. They had some time before all left for the outer isles, leaving the females to hatch and rear their chicks. This they do on a co-operative basis, so that often one eider can be seen with a dozen or more youngsters in her charge.

Perhaps two days spent next to a dead chick and its grieving mother while a summer gale blows itself out brings to the fore the more melancholy aspects of the north. These are a reality. It is true that life continues throughout the long winter, but the joy with which the return of the sun is greeted must have its grim counter-part in the souls of northerners. This is not a personal desponden-cy, something for which others might be held blameworthy, but a collective state of mind, shared by all. It is therefore spiced with an element of companionship and kindness.

However fanciful it may be to believe that the eiders understand this, to me their cries echo the bleaker side of life in the north and speak of a need to seek some kind of comfort. Is this melancholy, or just a statement of how nature works, that the best we, like the birds, can expect is a sense of loneliness shared with others?

That birds colour our experience is undeniable. Mostly they do so while leading lives of their own, in parallel to but quite separate from the lives of humans. This does not preclude the acceptance of crumbs, for example, or of fish guts thrown from trawlers. Fast food has its attractions for every species. Sometimes however birds and humans are drawn closer together, to the point where concessions have occasionally to be made by one side or the other.

We have vivid memories of the harbour at Dunmore East. It was perched at the entrance to the long inlet that leads to Waterford in Ireland, and was a small fishing port with no special facilities for yachts. Nor was it on our planned itinerary. We had intended to sail overnight from Cork to the Scilly Isles on a westerly wind, but found ourselves, as so often in those waters, with more wind than we wanted.

'Bunting' was already well reefed when I received the evening weather forecast of a possible force 7 and a shift in the direction of the wind to the south. I lost no time in changing course to 030° and heading for Dunmore East. That reduced the movement on the boat and made for a more comfortable night at sea, although the term was strictly comparative. By then we had larger waves to contend with, breaking on top so that some water came into the cockpit and even into the cabin.

By morning the wind had eased and we glided into the harbour in bright sunshine, to moor alongside the quay and dry out. It was a high quay, with a few vertical ladders leading to the top. In the next couple of days we were to have plenty of opportunities to climb these and see exactly where we had arrived, although one aspect of the place was clear already. This was the noise of hundreds of birds, all shouting at once throughout the day and on into the night 'Kitty WAKE, Kitty WAKE!'

The harbour was surrounded by steep cliffs where the kittiwakes had built their nests. The narrowest ledge was enough to accommodate these remarkable birds. There they anchored their nests with mud and clung to them to feed their chicks until the young were able to fly. Of all birds the kittiwake has to be the most optimistic and its chicks the calmest and least restive. Any major movement before it has learned how to use its wings is likely to prove fatal. Of course there were some casualties. Each morning the patient street cleaners of Dunmore East would collect the chicks that had fallen and carry them away in their carts.

There were other rocky cliffs along the coast which were used by kittiwakes, but nothing to indicate that they were preferred to those overlooking the harbour. The people of Dunmore East and their birds lived in harmony together, if harmony is a word that can be used in connection with the din that characterised that small and friendly town. Our unintended stay there serves to reiterate another of the great unspoken truths of yachting; that if you do not arrive at your planned destination you may well find that being some-where else is even more enjoyable.

If we had thought that the kittiwakes of Dunmore East nested close to their human neighbours, we were later to find birds that carried this process a stage further. In the tideless Baltic it is often the custom for yachts to moor in 'boxes'. These run along wooden jetties and are formed by sinking stout posts in the water to which stern lines can be attached while the boat noses in towards the jetty and moors so that the crew can step off the bow to go ashore. 'Sea Bear' carried a small folding ladder to facilitate the 'stepping' operation.

When these boxes had been designed for larger vessels the posts were placed farther from the jetty and were altogether stouter, the size of the tree trunks from which they had been made. Over time water would invade the exposed end grain and rot the wood, so that the tops of some posts became hollowed out. Then birds might see them as ideal nesting sites, well protected from predators.

So it was that in North Germany owners of large yachts or motor boats could be seen carefully lifting their mooring ropes over the tops of posts, complete with birds and eggs, in order to go out for a sail, and replacing them with equal care on their return. The birds did not seem to mind, although some of them clearly regarded 'Sea Bear' and her crew with suspicion.

The yacht harbour at Glücksburg on the Flensburger Förde was one of the most beautiful we had visited, surrounded by trees and, as yacht harbours go, extremely restful. We moored within sight of a post on which a pair of oystercatchers had established a nest. They had no reason to fear me. There was no way in which I could get close to their nest, but oystercatchers are exceedingly cautious and have their own stratagems for protecting their young. As I walked along the jetty the male bird would land in front of me and limp ahead, trailing one wing as if injured. Then, when he was sure I was at least three boats away, he would take to the air again. How he knew that I was a foreigner and not to be trusted, I cannot imagine.

The swallows of Arnis nested even closer to their human neighbours. They built nests underneath the wooden jetties. During the summer it was comforting to watch them, skimming over the water in their dozens, keeping the gnat population down. Towards the end of the season, as migration time approached, they would gather in the evening, side by side along the ropes which stretched from 'Sea Bear's' stern to the mooring posts, as if to remind us that we too would soon be heading south.

It has to be said that after two or three months spent cruising from port to port, relying on public showers and toilet facilities, living in our little boat in sunshine and in rain, we began to feel that the time had come to call a halt and seek home comforts once more. Naturally we hated to leave and to declare the season over, but neither did we wish to stay longer. And there were plans for next year to be made. Whether the swallows had similar thoughts I somehow doubt. They lived in a very different time frame. But their gathering along the mooring ropes presaged an event of some significance for them, more than simply chasing the gnats farther south.

Animals have joined the birds in lending colour to our memories of the north. Those creatures who lived ashore were naturally harder for us to see, since in most cases they were programmed to stay out of sight. In the water things were different. Seals had no inhibitions where humans were concerned, and would cheerfully follow our dinghy as we rowed to the shore. Although to say no inhibitions is going too far, for as soon as I lifted a camera they would disappear beneath the waves.

Scotland was the place to meet seals, as well as dolphins and the occasional whale. An abundance of fish in the waters around the Western Isles attracted these animals, as it did the plunging gannets. There were seals everywhere, in the water, basking on the rocks at the foot of a lighthouse, even in the harbour at Stornoway, where a large, old seal, his hunting days over, had found a retirement home, living off the scraps thrown out when the trawlers were unloaded.

We were able to observe him over several days as we lay uneasily in the fishing basin, sheltering from a severe summer gale. It was not a comfortable place to be, since we were there only by courtesy of the fishermen, who treated us kindly as they went about their business regardless of the abominable weather. This meant that we often had to shift moorings in the middle of the night, retrieving our ropes from the oily water and making fast to yet another rusty hull. In these conditions the old seal assumed a lugubrious air, as if to confirm that life here was always like this. And indeed the fishermen agreed that mostly it was so, winter and summer alike.

When the wind had eased a little we took a well-reefed 'Bunting' south to Loch Eport, to brave the swirling eddies of its narrow entrance channel and find the splendidly sheltered anchorage to which we had been directed by a doctor who sailed out of Stornoway and who knew every rock in the surrounding waters. Here we were able to watch seals at the other end of life's spectrum. A 'family' of youngsters were playing among the rocks just ahead of us, splashing the water about with their flippers and making a great deal of noise in the process. This was one of those rare places where a boat could lie all alone in a wilderness surrounded by crags with no company except the seals and the red deer that we had been told would appear from time to time on the skyline. We saw no deer but were more than content with our family of seals.

Land animals were indeed elusive in Scotland. On our trips ashore we found traces of deer and places where an otter had enjoyed a meal, but seldom met the creatures in the flesh. In fact I had come to believe that otters always brought their prey to the land to eat it, and that we were therefore unlikely to see any, when fate taught us otherwise.

We had entered the bay at Tobermory, admiring the sweep of brightly coloured houses round the harbour and looking for a place to anchor. This was difficult because the water close inshore was full of privately owned moorings and outside these a dredger was at work. Still further offshore the water was simply too deep. Eventually we found a sheltered spot at the far end of the bay in the Doirlinn narrows, and settled there to enjoy a fine evening.

As dusk came on, in the slow way it has in Scotland, I stood in the cockpit to have a last look around, as was my custom. All was quiet for a moment but then I heard strange noises coming from the water. Just astern of us an otter was hunting eels. He would take three huge breaths and then dive, to surface again with an eel in his jaws. Rather than waste time taking it ashore he ate it on the spot, turning it end on so that he could swallow it, then crunching it hungrily down. The noise of heavy breathing and rather messy chewing continued until it was almost dark. The otter took no notice of the boat or of me, concentrating on his work as if he were training for the eel eating championship of the Western Isles.

Once we had left Scotland and embarked on our cruise through the Baltic our contact with aquatic animals diminished. We found seals in Danish waters but by the time we had entered the Gulf of Bothnia they seemed to have vanished. This was disconcerting since 'Sea Bear' had been named after them. We knew they had become scarce but had expected to see a few at least. So our attempts to reach the bottom of the Gulf developed a secondary purpose, to find the seals.

Friends in the northern archipelago were adamant that they were there, and reported that fishermen were already complaining about their presence. We made special expeditions to the islands where they had been sighted but failed to find any. Then, when we had left the far north to begin our long journey home and were approaching the tiny harbour of Järnäshamn, we found them, dozens of them, on the rocks and in the water all around us. I doubt they had really come to say goodbye, but it seemed ironic that, after looking in vain for so long, we should finally meet so many.

As if in compensation for a shortage of sea-dwelling animals Sweden was rich in beasts of the four-footed kind. The first we noticed were the squirrels. These were red squirrels which had of course become hard to find in England. There the millions of conifer trees, stretching from the far south right up to Lapland enabled them to flourish. They appeared to be quite prepared to show themselves to us, albeit at a discreet distance. It was after all many centuries since squirrel skins were currency in those parts.

We had expected to see squirrels, although we were delighted to find them so forthcoming. The hedgehogs we met on the High Coast were more of a surprise. Ulvöhamn has a single street running through the village. In summer it is well used by visitors, all on foot for there are no cars on the island. Indeed this main street is too narrow for anything more than the small carts that bring goods from the quay to the few shops and restaurants the tourist trade sustains.

Walking along this street in the evening of our first visit I came face to face with a huge, silvery hedgehog who seemed quite unabashed to be sharing the road with people. It was quite the largest of these beasts I had ever seen, so it merited an entry in the ship's log. Then a year later we returned to Ulvöhamn with Katy who had joined us at Umeå for a tour of the High Coast. I was keen to show her the island and was walking through the village explaining how surprised I had been to find such an animal there, when another of them appeared at about the same spot, as if to confirm my story.

On reflection the amazement I felt at these meetings had three components. First was the size of the creatures, then there was the fact that they were consorting with humans in broad daylight, and finally there was the question of how hedgehogs managed to hibernate through so long a winter as was inevitable at a latitude of 63° north.

I suppose that all these elements are connected. To hibernate for such a time must require considerable body fat, which favours the larger animal. But this in turn means that the hedgehog has a lot of eating to do in the short summer. After that I can only speculate. The summer nights are so short that he cannot be purely nocturnal and must go about his business in daylight hours. I suspect that he also cannot afford to be too selective in his diet, and the proximity of people increases the possibility of additional food sources, just as it does for the bears in the Yosemite National Park.

Not that the Swedish summer is anything but bountiful. Short it may be, but long hours of sunshine encourage rapid growth. Plants which grow there, berries for example, grow faster and bigger than they do further south. And from what we observed the grubs and insects on which hedgehogs feed, keep pace with the plants, becoming for a while both sizeable and plentiful.

Larger animals were more shy, although deer were to be seen quite readily on the islands in the Stockholm archipelago. Indeed on Biskopsön, one of the outer isles, they were so numerous we were told that there had to be an annual cull. Swedish people seemed happy to have the deer in the woods around them, but it has to be said that this did not preclude a liking for venison.

The largest animal of all, the elk, was harder to find. So much so that for a time we thought he must be a mythical beast. When 'Sea Bear' first visited the Finnish island of Nauvo, Joy and I were invited home by Henrik Holmedahl and there cajoled into taking a sauna. At some sort of half-way point this involved Henrik and me standing naked in his garden, cooling off and waiting for an elk to appear at the fringe of the forest. It struck me at the time that you could not get much closer to nature than this, but sadly the elk did not oblige.

Everyone had stories of elk, of how dangerous it was if one stumbled into the path of your car at night, but for the most part we had no car and were confined to yacht harbours, so it is perhaps not surprising that over several years we failed to see a single one. Then, when we least expected it, we found our elk, in the most unlikely place we could have imagined.

'Sea Bear' was sailing through the inner channels of the Stockholm archipelago. She had a fair breeze, but it was accompanied by a steady, chilling rain. Joy had damaged a leg quite severely in a gale a few days before and had to rest for most of the time, which left me at the helm, cold and damp, picking our way through the islands as we headed south. It had so far been a depressing day.

We had just passed Dalarö when I spotted what looked like a fallen branch of a tree in the water ahead. On closer inspection it was a spread of antlers, under which could be seen the downturned snout of an elk. He was swimming across from Stora Rotholmen to haul himself out of the water on the island of Gålön. I took the time when we passed him and when he left the water on the far shore. Later I consulted the chart to measure the distance he had travelled, which was just under a mile. His speed through the water could then be calculated: it was approximately three knots, a very respectable figure for what at first appears to be a land animal.

I was delighted to find elk, as well as deer, so active on quite small islands so close to the city of Stockholm. It makes it easier to understand why many Swedish yachtsmen never venture outside the wonderful archipelago on their doorstep. There are so many channels to follow and there is so much there to see, changing its aspect all the time, as sunshine succeeds the rain or, on rare occasions, a mist gathers to make navigation through the rocks really 'interesting'.

In all we spent many days among the islands and, with the help of Swedish friends, explored places well off the beaten track. This certainly helped us to understand their enthusiasm and even, for a brief while, to share in it, but it could not make us Stockholmers. For us the archipelago was one stage on our journey, not an end in itself. However long it took we were always passing through and on towards the open sea where we belonged, just as we were doing on the day we met our elk.

None of the birds or beasts we saw served to represent the north to us. That would be asking too much of them. What they did was to add another layer to our understanding and to enrich the memories we took away with us. Yet some came close to symbolism in the light they shone on certain aspects of life there, as the eiders did on the gentle melancholy that underlies the joy of summer. No beast could match this, but one did carry an air, not of melancholy, but of mystery, and that was the *skogshare* or forest hare.

Hares have for centuries appeared to possess some element of magic. Those we saw in the north were of a mottled brown and grey colour. Seeing them against the scrub and boulders on the shore was not easy for, once they felt that they were observed, they would freeze and make themselves invisible, merging into the landscape so that if you did not know they were there you would never have noticed them.

For all that they were not unduly timid, and seemed to enjoy watching us as much as we enjoyed watching them. Once they had decided that we were harmless they revelled in their ability to appear and disappear at will, standing stock still amongst the rocks that had been rolled down by glaciers long before the first sailor anchored off those shores.

CHAPTER SEVEN

A World of Grey

I T MIGHT BEGIN WITH NO MORE than a thickening of the air, a blurring of the horizon, or with something much more obvious, a rolling bank of mist moving towards you over the water. Often it was heard before it was seen. You woke to an oppressive silence with none of the usual sounds of morning. On a mooring or at anchor, the noise of birds calling to each other or scurrying about the deck would be replaced by a slow drip, drip of water from the boom on to the cabin top. Then you would look out on a damp, grey world, other boats around you vague shapes in the mist, sounds of activity muffled as their crews too took stock of a dismal day.

If you chose to put to sea in such conditions you might find yourself passing a long line of gulls standing side by side on the harbour wall, hunched and unhappy. They would look at you as you went by as if asking the inevitable question: 'Do you think you should?' For the greyness into which you were heading was a form of sense deprivation, and as such a rightful cause of unease in humans as well as in birds.

Today's sailor may elect to ignore such qualms. He has his satellite navigator to show him where he is and, in larger craft, his radar to warn him of hazards – always provided that he has someone spare to sit in front of it. But this is to disregard the fact that in fog large vessels equipped with all such gadgets, and manned by professional seamen, have smashed into each other or impaled themselves on rocks.

In our earlier years at sea we had only a compass, an echo

sounder and the occasional RDF bearing to guide us, which made fog rather more dangerous. Yet some of my most satisfying and enjoyable memories emerge from that world of grey. This is not to say that the experience was quite so enjoyable at the time: the concentration demanded by this type of sailing often precluded that. With one of the senses severely impaired the others were sometimes strained to the limit. It is however beyond doubt that sailing through fog was 'interesting' in the Scandinavian sense of the word.

To anyone devoted to the art of navigation it provided the ultimate challenge. You calculated the strength and direction of tidal streams, set a course to minimise any dangers, used every means available to check your position, with the exception of that vital one now denied to you, and discovered in the end whether you were right or wrong. There was no way of making those minor corrections which you made very sensibly in the normal course of events whenever your eyes told you that you were liable to miss your target. 'Cheating' in that way was impossible before the advent of electronic positioning systems.

Naturally we avoided situations where failure was likely to prove fatal. Crossing really busy shipping lanes or making a landfall on a broken shore littered with isolated rocks were unacceptable risks. That still left many instances where, with care, it was safe enough to venture out and put our navigational skills to the test. In doing so we honed the basic techniques we had already learned and discovered others that were not in any textbook.

Our adventures in the Moray Firth will serve to illustrate how this might happen. Over the years we acquired a small portfolio of unconventional and at times opportunistic methods of fixing our position at sea. These included observation of the trail of rubbish thrown out by cross channel ferries and of the flight path of helicopters attending offshore rigs. Here, in fog and unable to use our eyes to any effect we were to discover navigation by bird song.

It was in 1982 that Joy and I sailed from Norway to Scotland, accompanied by our old friend Tom. 'Bunting' had given us a comparatively stress-free passage, but we were glad of a day or two in Fraserburgh to relax and restock with fresh food. The plan was then to sail along the southern shore of the Moray Firth to Inverness, cross Scotland by the Caledonian Canal and establish a base on the west coast for the following winter. To accomplish this a stop at Lossiemouth was indicated, from where we might be able to reach Inverness on just one tide.

Lossiemouth was crowded and far from comfortable, but this did not matter unduly as we were due to leave at 05.00. At dawn, for a busy fishing port, the place seemed strangely quiet. Thick fog covered everything. It was one of those mornings when a decision to leave harbour had to be carefully weighed. Just how much thought we gave it I cannot now recall. Certainly the prevailing weather pattern gave hope that the mist would lift later in the day. Then the southern shore of the Moray Firth was for much of the way ideal for navigation in fog. That is to say it sloped gently with fairly straight and regular depth contours, so that we could run along a line of soundings with no risk of meeting really large ships. Nevertheless I suspect that I was seeing that fog as a challenge to our developing skills in navigation and one that I was eager to accept. The borderline between actions that are necessary to advance knowledge and experience and those that are merely rash is itself sometimes shrouded in mist.

Not everyone shared my confidence. The piers at Lossiemouth were at most 19 metres apart. As we centred 'Bunting' between them they could just be seen on either side. A voice hailed us from one of them, asking politely if we were sure we knew what we were doing. My cheerful and positive reply concealed a profound hope that the mist would clear before we reached the more difficult parts of our voyage.

Of course it did not. We motored carefully along, just inside the 10 metre depth contour, blowing our hand held foghorn from time to time but meeting no other vessels. By 10.00 another decision had to be made. My dead reckoning put us somewhere to the east of Nairn. Exactly where we could not tell. For the last few hours navigation had been easy, but once past Nairn there were serious problems to be faced.

In the first place White Ness Sand jutted out into the Firth and was quite steep-to. That I believed we could manage, but through it had been dredged a channel to McDermott Base, from which huge oil-rigs were towed on their way to the North Sea. I did not want to meet one of those in fog. A day or so later, in clearer weather, we saw one of them being very slowly moved by no fewer than four tugs, an incredible tangle of metal, ships and towing cables.

As it was we did what seemed prudent, and anchored in about four metres to wait for the fog to clear. If it did that quickly enough we could continue: if not we would have to put into Nairn. That thought did not please me because Nairn was a small harbour that for the most part dried out, but it was our one port of refuge on this particular journey.

In the silence that ensued when our anchor cable had been paid out and the motor stopped we gave some thought to the question of where exactly we were in this grey world. My estimated position had been calculated on a fail-safe basis inspired by the need to keep to the east of Nairn. It was as near to the harbour as we could have reached if the tide had pushed us as hard as it could at its maximum strength. It was quite possible that we had not come so far.

Tom was the first to provide a clue. His ears are phenomenally keen. 'I can hear breakers, inshore and astern of us.' Yes, they were there, but with my own ears now fully tuned I could hear something else. It was a bird, and its twittering trill took me back to our days on the Broads, when we moored among willows and reed-beds, not in a damp, grey nothingness somewhere off the coast of Scotland.

Joy listened hard and confirmed my diagnosis: 'A reed bunting!' Now although we had named the boat in which we were standing after that particular bird, we had not expected to meet one here. It was calling from a point to the west of Tom's breakers, and it was safe to assume that it was not sitting on a bare sand dune to sing its song. Reed buntings need reeds, or something very like them.

So we set about trying to locate reeds on the chart. All it showed

was a line of dunes along the coast called 'The Bar', but it did indicate breakers at one point. The Admiralty Pilot for the north coast
of Scotland spoke of The Bar as 'covered by coarse grass in places.'
It also added, prophetically, that it was 'not easy to distinguish from
seaward.'

Now we had breakers, a possible location for the bird and, of
course, the depth of water under us to fix our position. It was clear
that we had not reached my fail-safe point, but were still some
distance to the east. As the sun was from time to time trying to
break through we decided on an early lunch, in the hope that the
fog would soon clear. About mid-day a ghostly yacht appeared, out
for a weekend sail from Nairn. Her skipper confirmed we were
about three miles from the harbour. There was now no choice but
to go there if we did not want to spend a night in the Moray Firth.
There was also no point in further delay, since the visibility had
again closed down and what had been a hint of sunlight had now
vanished.

So on we went, keeping as close as possible to the unseen shore
in order not to miss the harbour when we arrived there. I felt that
a course somewhere between the two and three metre depth contours should serve, but there was a moment of anxiety when the
echo sounding dropped suddenly to only one metre and we felt a
bump as our keel rode over an obstacle, probably a sewage outlet
pipe. Then in an instant the harbour wall was in front of us and the
beach close to our port side. We had to turn sharply to seaward to
follow the pier out to the harbour entrance.

Once inside we were advised to moor alongside a concrete wall
near the harbour steps. It was by then 12.50 and near the time of
high water. For the first time that day we felt we could relax.

Our peaceful afternoon was soon to be interrupted. As the tide
fell it became clear that the solid wall to which we had made fast was
not so solid after all. With the fall in the level of the water a large,
hollow cavern appeared, into which 'Bunting's' hull threatened to
tumble, with predictable and disastrous consequences for the mast
and rigging. It was already too late to move, so I rushed around

the harbour to see if anyone had a plank that we could use to span the gap.

No one had, but some fishermen kindly lent us two of their very large fenders, which we gratefully lowered into place. When I asked how I could return them when the time came for us to leave they replied: 'Don't worry. When you go just tie them to the fence.'

Nairn was, in every way, a most friendly place. We sat in the clubhouse that evening chatting with local sailors and watching the mist clear. Not all of the yachts that had ventured out on that foggy day had returned to harbour. One or two had missed the entrance and could be seen stranded on the beach. They would be there until the next high tide, but at least their crews could relax in the bar in the meantime.

In retrospect the day had served to boost my confidence in fog navigation, at least when bird-aided, as well as in human nature. It had however left me resolved to avoid drying harbours whenever possible. We set out early the next morning, sailing past that formidable oil-rig under tow, to be greeted by seals as we found the entrance to the Caledonian Canal. Fine weather had returned. We commenced a transit of Scotland with the wind miraculously behind us and the sun shining brightly over Loch Ness and the hills round about.

Over the succeeding two years Scotland was to provide me with abundant experience of fog, as well as of gales, rain and even snow. There were also perfect sailing days, when the scenery blazed green in sunshine and the water was so clear that you could stand in the bow of your little ship and follow the chain down link by link to the anchor embedded in sand. It was a place of extremes and changes could be sudden and severe.

Our next expedition in fog was a crossing of the Minch to the Outer Hebrides. This time we had no bird to help us, although guillemots, puffins and gannets were there in quantity. Paradoxically the calm, glassy sea that accompanied the mist made it easier to see them, as well as the dolphins which frisked around and under our boat. But they were not there to show us the way.

In fact some care had to be taken in setting a course, since the direct route to our destination was not safe in poor visibility. We were crossing from Badachro on Loch Gairloch to Loch Shell on the island of Lewis. Unfortunately the coastline around Loch Shell was deeply indented and strewn with rocks, hardly an ideal landfall. Furthermore a direct course would take us close to the Shiant Islands, of which the pilot books had nothing good to say. But north of Loch Shell there was a long line of unbroken cliff, steep-to and with no offshore hazards. So the plan was to 'aim off' and head for that cliff, knowing that when we met it we would have to turn to port and let it guide us home.

A patch of shallow water to the east of the Shiants was identified by our echo sounder to confirm that we were on course. Then in mid-afternoon a fair wind filled our sails, although the mist became even thicker. We must have passed within three miles of the Shiant Islands but saw nothing of them whatsoever.

Without warning the grey ahead of us became black, and in seconds a wall of cliff appeared. We now had to beat a short way southward to find Loch Shell and the anchorage at Tob Lemrevay. That part of our plan had proved highly successful, but our luck was not to hold.

We had intended to reprovision at Tob Lemrevay before sailing down the Hebridean chain of islands. Tob Lemrevay however turned out to be not a village but a settlement of separate crofts, each with a stack of peat outside, a few sheep or sometimes a cow, and a black and white dog. The inhabitants wore long coats that were almost a uniform, augmented on Sundays by a Bible tucked under one arm.

They greeted us most civilly, but it was clear that for supplies we would have to go north, back along the coast to Stornoway. And so we did, which meant an extended stay in the harbour there while a severe gale raged and we came to learn something of a way of life which combined extreme bigotry with much human kindness, and seemed to belong to a different century altogether.

We had intended to leave Scotland the next year, but it was to prove not easy to escape from those fascinating waters, or from the mists which had, if anything, added to their interest for us. From the outset we ran into difficulties. Joy became ill with a painful rheumatic condition which was ultimately stabilised, but put her out of action for the whole of the next sailing season. If 'Bunting' were to come south I would need help from elsewhere. This led to the evolution of a plan designed both to get our boat to Falmouth and to give good friends of mine the chance of a sail in Celtic waters.

The intention was for Andy, a competent sailor whose early career had been with one of the more drastic branches of the Armed Forces, to travel north with me and help take the boat to a harbour on the west coast of Ireland. We could not be sure how far we would get in the two weeks he could spare, but resolved to stop at a place with reasonably good rail or air connections. Then Andy would return home while Tom came out to join me for the second leg of the journey.

In retrospect I am inclined to think that at this stage of my sailing career I was becoming over confident and over ambitious. Perhaps it was the successful voyage across from Norway that started this trend, or possibly just frustration at holidays that were generous by business standards, but never seemed to yield enough time to do all that we might wish.

The first corrective to my optimism came all too soon. Andy and I had sailed just over 50 miles and were entering Port Ellen on the island of Islay under power, when our propeller struck an obstacle of some kind. The shock was transmitted up the propeller shaft to the gearbox, with the result that everything came to a juddering halt. It was no great problem to hoist sail and find a mooring inside the harbour, but I was not keen to explore the west coast of Ireland without an engine. There seemed no alternative but to return to the boatyard at Ardfern on Loch Craignish for repairs.

It took us two days to get back, drifting northward in light airs and working our way across the strong currents that run through the northern part of the Sound of Jura. Sadly for Andy, that was the end of his cruise. The boatyard could not obtain the necessary parts and eventually he had to catch a train home, leaving me to fret and fume at the enforced delay.

Finally Tom came to the rescue, arriving off the night sleeper at Glasgow laden with a new gearbox and propeller shaft. Three days later 'Bunting' set out once more. So much time had now been lost that we would have to travel by the shortest route, down the east coast of Ireland, rather than embark on the circumnavigation I had planned. We had charts for only the northern part of the journey and would have to buy others on the way.

Our first stop was the island of Gigha, and it was here that the next hitch occurred. Our paraffin cooker suffered a fractured pipe and began to spray fuel around the cabin. Clearly it was unusable. In a half-hearted way I tried to persuade Tom that cooking was not really necessary: we had a full tank of water, a plentiful supply of tinned food and a well-stocked beer locker. Tom was however adamant. He had not carried large chunks of machinery hundreds of miles to be denied his morning cup of tea. Something would have to be done.

At this point a short digression is indicated. It was, after all, 1984. We were not sailing with Erskine Childers in his 'Dulcibella'. So why was I using paraffin when bottled gas was the norm and freely available? The answer lies in the type of sailing I intended, which involved passing from one country to another, and often wintering overseas. Different countries had different types of gas cylinders and even different types of gas. We had used gas in 'Bugle' and had discovered just what difficulties that could cause. Paraffin could at that time be obtained almost anywhere, and was also much easier to store.

The logic was sound but the type of cooker installed in 'Bunting' was prone to fractured pipes. For 'Sea Bear' we specified the wonderful Taylor stove, old-fashioned and requiring spirit to pre-heat the burners, but fundamentally reliable. It was also a thing of beauty with its solid enamelled black top and gleaming brass and stainless steel body. It is true that the brass needed polishing, and on our longer cruises one day would have to be dedicated to dismantling the stove, clearing any blockages and perhaps changing a burner, but what are rainy days for?

None of this could help us at Gigha. It was already evening when I rowed ashore in the faint hope of finding a source of heat for the remainder of our voyage. My pessimism was quite unfounded. Emergencies of the kind we were experiencing were nothing new to people living on islands off the Scottish coast, and their willingness to aid mildly distressed mariners was exemplary. I returned to the boat with a full cylinder of gas and an attachment that could be fitted to the top of it to make a primitive cooker. The evening was suddenly bathed in sunshine.

As the voyage progressed we found a place to store our new acquisition when it was cool, but the only place where it could be used was in the middle of the cabin. With any movement on the boat the cylinder had to be gripped between the cook's legs so long as the burner was alight, and we both became quite skilled at this.

The next day we set out to make what we hoped would be a fast passage to Falmouth. The omens were not good. Fog closed in to make the Mull of Kintyre a dim outline to port as we headed south. The radar reflector was hoisted for the crossing to Ireland as some shipping could be expected in the North Channel, but the short passage from one country to the other passed without incident. We closed the coast and groped our way into Red Bay to anchor off the beach, still in thick mist.

On reflection, arriving on this particular shore in a rubber dinghy from a boat shrouded in fog may not have been the wisest move. This was Northern Ireland in troubled times, but we were innocents abroad, unaware of local conditions and of course came to no harm. It was however a depressing experience. The small town nearby had a dilapidated air. The police station was surrounded by a high wall topped with ample quantities of barbed wire. The people we encountered were surly and suspicious, quite unlike the Irish folk we were to meet further south.

We were glad to creep away the next day, still in mist which persisted until the evening. Then it cleared to enable us to make an overnight passage to Howth, some 120 miles south. This was an excellent place to stop, although we were there for no more than half a day. It was necessary to call in there because we had now run out of charts. The only chart we could buy covered the whole of the southern part of the Irish Sea. This was quite adequate for passage making but on too small a scale for feeling our way along the coast in fog. At the time however visibility was good, so in the afternoon we set off again for Arklow and a good night's sleep.

The morning saw us once more in thick mist. Time was pressing but the thought of finding our way between the sandbanks with the aid of a chart that required a magnifying glass in constant use made us hesitate. By mid-day the tide had turned in our favour and the decision was made to go. Tom remarked on the lugubrious expression of the gulls that watched us leaving harbour. He did not share my enthusiasm for fog navigation, although his acute sense of hearing was a most valuable weapon in our limited armoury and had proved its use in guiding us to the whistle buoys that marked a passage through the shallows of this particular coast line.

On this stage we were travelling parallel to the beach and so close that I could almost have shaken hands with the men who were walking their dogs along the foreshore. Then the mist thinned to enable us to find our way into Rosslare, where we anchored off the ferry port to prepare for the final leg of our voyage, a passage of 180 miles to Falmouth.

By 07.20 the next morning we had stowed our improvised cooker and were under way. Rosslare was no place to linger. The mist stayed with us until mid-day, when we picked up a light, westerly breeze, which strengthened as night fell, to the point where I had to take in a reef. By the time we were approaching Falmouth the wind had shifted to the north west and increased still further, to give us an exhilarating beat into the harbour. At least that is how I remember it, although Tom claimed that on one occasion he had emerged from the cabin to find 'Bunting' precisely on course and me with a firm hand on the tiller, but with my eyes tightly shut.

Certainly we were tired. Over the previous week we had averaged 58 miles, or about 12 hours of sailing time, a day, a good proportion of it in fog. That was far from leisurely cruising. And Tom had been cheated of a chance to see Ireland, almost any part of Ireland, let alone the mysterious west coast I had promised him. So why, I wonder, did we both feel so pleased with life?

That forced march down the Irish Sea represented something of a pinnacle in my experience of sailing in fog. Of course there was more to come. In 'Sea Bear' Joy and I were to cross the Baltic and the Gulf of Bothnia in visibility every bit as poor. We were to sail among the rocks of the Channel Islands and through the Chenal du Four with its vicious tidal streams, in a clinging mist. But 'Sea Bear' had been fitted with Decca, so we were able to 'cheat' and correct our course if the position that instrument gave us was not as planned.

Naturally I was glad to do so. There is no doubt that electronic navigation made our lives easier. Nevertheless it could not provide the sheer fun that stemmed from using depth contours, black cliffs, shallow patches, bird song and Tom's ears to find our way.

Nor could Decca have made sailing in fog a safe activity. Quite apart from the danger from large ships there was the fact that I was using an instrument accurate to about a quarter of a mile, and at times to no more than half a mile. On the open sea an error of a quarter of a mile was of little consequence. Approaching a rock strewn coast it might well have proved fatal.

It was also the case that while I was busy pencilling Decca positions on the chart, Joy was left alone in the cockpit, with only one pair of eyes. It was not so easy to steer a compass course, keep an eye on the echo sounder and maintain a 360° lookout all at the same time. If something should loom out of the mist there would be only a few seconds to identify what it was or to take evasive action if necessary.

So we tried to keep our older, proven techniques ready for use when required. This meant giving serious thought to the question posed by those gloomy gulls on foggy mornings: whether or not to put to sea. Was the visibility likely to improve and, if so, when? What were the hazards inherent in the course planned? Were there any natural features, buoys or lighthouses on the way that might serve to confirm our position?

A damp, cold morning when all is quiet in the harbour and the world around you is lost in grey does not provide the most encouraging background to decisions of this kind. Yet often we decided to go, and never regretted it. The choice was in essence only one of many that navigators have to make, none of them without some element of risk. In a life where much has of necessity to be done at the behest of others, to be able to make such a choice is a privilege to be savoured.

CHAPTER EIGHT

Wind and Waves

S AILING WOULD BE A MORE PLEASANT ACTIVITY if the wind would only behave itself. Ideally we would have very little of it when leaving an overnight mooring, then it would increase to a steady force 3 or 4 from a direction abaft the beam, so that we made a minimum of leeway and bowled along at a brisk pace with hardly any rolling, pitching or lurching about. Of course when we reached our destination it would immediately die away to allow us to moor neatly and without fuss.

In reviewing my memories of cruising with Joy I have tried to recall days like that, without success. True, we may have had ideal conditions for a few hours, but seldom, if ever, for a whole day. The problem with wind, at least in what might be loosely described as North West Europe, is that there is either too little of it or too much.

Now is the time to talk about those occasions on which there was too much. We did not experience very many of these because, if heavy weather had been forecast, I generally stayed in harbour. It might not have been brave, or even pleasant, to sit in a small cabin with the windows misting up, while rain beat on the deck and wind howled in the rigging, but it seemed preferable to what might await us outside.

Nevertheless forecasts are not always reliable, so there were times when we were caught out in gale or near-gale conditions. If that description seems a trifle vague, it will have to remain so. One of the more difficult things is to estimate wind strength accurately. Nowadays there are mast-head instruments that purport to do this.

We never fitted one of these, largely because I wanted to let my burgee fly freely at the top of the mast, so we relied on the descriptions given in the Beaufort scale and on experience. However, what instruments do show is that wind seldom remains steady for more than a few seconds. What tends to stick in the mind is the strength of gusts rather than the sustained average force of the wind around you.

It is therefore not surprising that yachtsmen are inclined to over-estimate the strength of the wind they have endured, rather as fishermen can inflate the size of the fish that escaped them. A question you are sometimes asked by the truly inexperienced is: 'What is the strongest wind you have sailed in?' An honest, if unsatisfactory, answer might be: 'I'm not sure.' It could be more helpful to query the relevance of the question itself.

The whole business of handling rough weather at sea depends not just on the strength of the wind but also on its direction and the kind of waves it produces. I have sailed happily in force 8 up and down stretches of coastline, when the wind came from the shore and the sea remained relatively calm. Yet winds of not much more than force 6, coming at you from across a couple of hundred miles of open water can create problems for small boats, especially for boats with crews that are neither numerous nor young.

It gets more difficult when such winds meet strong tidal streams, or blow over shallow seas to create waves that are ragged and steep. Then there is the effect of gusts that may strike suddenly at speeds far greater than the average, and the existence of waves that occasionally, and quite at random, roll in at twice the height of those before them. Taking these factors into consideration, it becomes clear that that there is no simple yardstick for measuring the seriousness of weather at sea.

That would hold true even in bright sunshine. However what is tough but manageable in clear visibility may become much more difficult in blinding rain or at night. In darkness it is all too easy to believe that the waves are larger than they are in fact, and of course it is harder to steer so as to minimise their effect.

Our own actions naturally make life easier or otherwise in rough weather. Well-manned racing yachts, their crews fired with competitive enthusiasm, may relish a stiff beat to windward in such conditions. We have been more inclined to look for a safe harbour somewhere downwind. The going then is much easier, although it carries the danger that the full force of the wind may not be appreciated until a change of direction becomes necessary.

In spite of all these variables there was one practical indicator that we took to heart. The standard Beaufort wind scale at one point speaks of a sea condition where 'white foam from braking waves begins to be blown in streaks along the direction of the wind.' This is force 7 or near gale strength. Neither Joy nor I enjoyed watching those streaks of foam develop.

However hard we tried to avoid it there were inevitably times when we were caught out by unexpected storms. From a Darwinian point of view this was just as well, for how were we to learn how to cope with this sort of weather without experience? It was vital that we came to understand what it took to handle the ship and ourselves in such circumstances.

Looking back there were two categories of heavy weather in wait for us, one the short sharp squall where wind speeds might be high but only for a short time, either because the wind eased or because we quickly found refuge in harbour, the other the prolonged blow when we had to adjust to hours of misery before finding a safe haven.

The former we met quite early on, when we were sailing 'Bugle'. We were on passage down the English Channel. For the first leg of the voyage, from Harwich to Boulogne, we had as crew our daughter Katy and our friend and next door neighbour, Mike. He was a dinghy sailor and this trip was intended to provide him with a taste of sea sailing.

A day of light winds took us across the Thames Estuary. We had the option of continuing overnight to Boulogne, but a forecast of fog prompted us to put into Ramsgate for a few hours sleep. Joy and I were also a little concerned about Mike. He had appeared to enjoy the trip so far but had shown signs of queasiness in the lop of the estuary seas.

He and all the crew seemed fit enough the next morning. We left early to catch the west-going tide. There was very little wind, so we were under power until I stopped the motor to listen to the 06.33 forecast. It was not good news. Westerly winds eventually reaching force 7 were predicted. What we had at the time was no more than a good sailing breeze, and we should be in Boulogne by mid-day, so it seemed safe to continue.

Unfortunately the forecasters were a little out in their timing. The bad weather came on us almost immediately and with the wind pushing against a strong tidal stream we soon had much bigger seas to contend with. I had changed to a smaller foresail and taken in a precautionary reef while we were still in the shelter of the land, so progress was fast and not too uncomfortable until we closed the French coast.

On the approach to Boulogne a cross-Channel ferry came up astern of us, an impressive sight with spray breaking over the bridge. It did however present us with a problem. It seemed desirable to turn out of the ship's path, and early enough to let the skipper see that we were safely clear. We had a sandbank to starboard so I turned towards the coast where there was more room to manoeuvre. When the ship had passed this left us with a hard slog out again to reach the entrance to the harbour.

The waves by then were so steep that we lost the wind in the troughs and had to regain control each time we came up again. Mike had put aside any suggestion of seasickness and was thoroughly enjoying himself. All I could do was advise everyone to hold on tight for a rough and very wet ride into Boulogne.

We stayed in Boulogne for some days while the gale raged and the lifeboat made frequent trips out to collect those who had not been as lucky as us. We were conscious that we had made harbour in the nick of time. A few more hours at sea in those conditions could have proved a most unhappy experience. It was an object lesson in how quickly a storm of this kind might develop from an almost flat calm, and how, admittedly on rare occasions, forecasters could fail to predict it sufficiently far in advance.

In thundery conditions a squall may not be predicted at all, and the yachtsman is not going to be any wiser than the professional forecaster. When black clouds gather the outcome is just as likely to be a sullen, vertical downpour on to a glassy sea as a really vicious gust of wind. Some sixteen years after our Boulogne gale we had both these phenomena in a single day.

We were on a passage of some fifty miles from the lovely harbour of Ratan to Skelleftehamn, further north in the Gulf of Bothnia, sailing close-hauled in a moderate easterly breeze. Some time after mid-day the sky grew very dark. A light flurry of wind prompted me to take in a reef in anticipation of trouble to come. That was enough to produce a flat calm, so we motored through the rain, carrying our reefed mainsail like a line of washing.

After nearly three hours of this the weather brightened again and we were once more sailing. I was either extremely cautious or simply lazy, but I left the reef in place, distrusting what was proving to be a fickle day. In the evening the thunderclouds gathered again, and this time there was no warning at all. The wind changed direction and hit us at full gale strength. The boom came crashing over and I was knocked off my feet, having to emerge from beneath the tiller before control could be regained. Then 'Sea Bear' took off like a rocket, running before the wind until the squall subsided half an hour later.

Other yachts were not so fortunate. On the following day we were visited in Skelleftehamn by the skipper of an older, wooden boat who had also experienced that squall offshore. He had been dismasted and was now in some trouble with his insurance company. The problem was that no strong winds had been forecast, and that in Skelleftehamn there was no official record of any wind at all that day. So the insurers were naturally sceptical of a reported dismasting. At least I could confirm the reality of the squall and provide an extract from 'Sea Bear's' log book to use in evidence if required. That was the shortest gale we ever saw, but the fact that it had caused damage did not surprise us. The sudden change of wind direction and the violence of the gusts that hit us would have put a strain on any yacht's rigging. 'Sea Bear' was of course stronger than most but I was glad I had left that reef in place.

In the years between these short sharp incidents, we were given the opportunity to discover how we might react to more sustained periods of heavy weather. The first chance came in the year following the dash that Tom and I had made down the Irish Sea to Falmouth. 'Bunting' had wintered happily enough in the West Country, but now a fresh decision had to be made. Were we to head east to complete our imperfect circumnavigation, or should we take advantage of our new base to return and see something of Ireland?

The choice was compounded by the fact that, although Joy had recovered from the worst of her illness, she was hardly at full strength. And it was a long way from Falmouth to the south coast of Ireland. To strengthen the crew for that crossing we attempted to recruit a friend, another Vega sailor. However a prolonged spell of bad weather ruined our plans and left us to choose between going on our own or abandoning Ireland altogether. Somehow, after the frustrations of the previous year, we felt we could not let the opportunity slip. We decided to go, recognising that I might have to do more helming than usual. Just how much more I was soon to discover.

To avoid the possibility of two nights at sea I decided to sail to the Scilly Isles and anchor overnight. Then we could contemplate what for us would be a routine passage to Crosshaven, starting in the morning, sailing through the night and arriving the following afternoon.

For this we required a spell of settled weather. When it arrived we set off in a calm to find a delightful anchorage in New Grimsby Sound. The only disturbing factor was the swell that met us on rounding the north coast of St. Martins. With so light a wind this could only be the result of weather farther out in the Atlantic. It served as a reminder of just how exposed the seas were in this part of the world.

Our departure from New Grimsby was idyllic. The sun shone, the water was crystal clear and even the anchor came up bright and clean from its bed in the sand. All seemed set fair. As we sailed north fluffy clouds could be seen on the horizon, marking the position of each of the Scilly Isles and even of Cornwall, like an inverted chart in the sky. The forecast had been for a south westerly wind of about force 4, absolutely ideal for our purpose.

By evening this had been modified and force 4 to 5 was being forecast for the night ahead, still quite acceptable but as much as we wanted to see. Nevertheless the evening passed peacefully and when whisky time came we drank to 'Bunting's' first 5,000 miles.

A fine sail through the hours of darkness was followed by a depressing dawn. It had started to rain, visibility had become quite poor, it was very definitely blowing force 5 and the seas were growing larger with every minute. A glimpse of the Kinsale Head Gas field from the top of a wave showed that we had been set too far to the east, so we altered course to windward to ensure that we would not be swept right past Cork Harbour.

Our automatic steering gear, one of the earlier versions, was not up to these conditions and had to be disconnected. I soon began to appreciate its difficulties; the helm was already quite hard to hold. Joy took over the steering while I went on deck to reef the mainsail. It was not a pleasant excursion.

From this point onwards entries in the ship's log became sparse. I was at the helm most of the time, while Joy was finding the movement below a strain on her still rheumatic limbs. The wind had clearly reached force 6 and was gusting higher. Waves were large but long, a real Atlantic swell. They also developed a tendency to break on top, with a most unpleasant hissing sound.

Navigation naturally became less precise. I came to appreciate the sight we had had of the Gas Fields. The path of helicopters, often heard rather than seen, to and from the rigs gave us some help. Assuming they came from somewhere near Cork, so long as their path was to starboard of us there was no risk of our being swept too far to the east. Our compass course was naturally set to avoid this possibility, but I was very aware that in the kind of weather we were experiencing where you are pointing is not necessarily where you are going: leeway can be far greater than normal.

There was also our faithful RDF set. Joy could take the tiller for a few minutes while I obtained a bearing on the Old Head of Kinsale. A series of these confirmed that we were approaching the coast of Ireland, although at what point could not be determined. So with the Old Head to port and the helicopters to starboard we closed the unseen shore.

I had by then been at the helm for some hours and was beginning to tire. There was little to see except the compass that I was trying to hold steady on course. At one stage this began to appear as a jellyfish, floating before my eyes. It took a little while to shake myself back to reality. That would really not do. Experience shows that concentrating the gaze too narrowly has a hypnotic effect. It is better to move the eyes around from time to time, and essential in fact if you are the only one on watch.

Perhaps even more important is the frame of mind that you adopt. There are occasions, mercifully few, when it is necessary to switch to what I think of as 'endurance mode'. Then how you got to be in a difficult situation means nothing. And neither does the anticipation of a safe harbour and much needed sleep. All that matters is doing the simple tasks that are required, forever if need be.

Then land was sighted through the gloom. Neither of us could tell what part of the coast lay ahead. There were no recognisable landmarks, but at least it was Ireland. Another bearing on the Old Head of Kinsale showed how near we were to the shore. The signal was so clear that we must have been quite close to the lighthouse, and indeed the water appeared calmer, so we were probably getting some shelter from the Old Head itself.

All that was left was a run downwind along the coast until we could identify the entrance to Cork Harbour. Of course that took us out into rougher water once more. As we ran between the headlands that guarded the expanse of water inside Joy stood in the companionway looking at the rolling seas following us in, towering

A new propeller
fitted at Kappeln

'Sea Bear' on the Orwell.
Picture by Mike Emmerson

Joy sets her
cruising chute

Gieslau Lock,
where we saw a
pair of cuckoos

The Eider River near Friedrichstadt

Plastic cut from 'Sea Bear's' propeller in the Gulf of Gdansk

Ingmarsö, 'Sea Bear's' home in the Stockholm archipelago

Simphamn, near Umeå

At anchor off Biskopsön

Halsön

Renskär in the far north

Joy and the author at Lövskär.

Picture by Pär Bäckström, NSD

Sweden's west coast near Marstrand

Greetsiel

Concarneau, under the walls of La Ville Close

Trieux river, near Lézardrieux

above my head as I sat at the helm. There was however now no need to worry. By then I had recovered from my hallucinatory bout of tiredness and was delighting in our arrival. It had been a fast passage, if one that had revealed all too clearly the difficulties faced by a weak crew in weather of that kind.

Just how weak a crew were we? I have wondered about that in the years following our Irish expedition. Physically I suspect we were as about as weak at that time as we could be without inviting disaster. A third crew member might well have eased the strain on us. Yet somehow it seems wrong to think of a crew as a collection of individuals. That is acceptable, indeed desirable, ashore, but at sea a crew can and should become something else, a unity, almost an organism in which personal idiosyncrasies are subordinated to the needs of the ship.

If this is true then temperament matters even more than sailing skills. A crew member who buckles under pressure or even one who is, as my friend Andy would say, 'too brave' threatens this concept: a domineering skipper can destroy it altogether. Joy and I had reached a point where we could rely on each other completely. In that respect we had become a crew strong enough to cope with the occasional bad day or bad night at sea.

It has to be said that really bad days were rare. The voyage to Ireland was in 1985 and our next testing time did not come until 1990. Overall it seems that the more serious episodes in our sailing lives were at intervals of at least five years. This may indicate either the extent of my timidity, or the general accuracy of the weather forecasts we received.

In 1990 we were sailing out of the Gulf of Bothnia towards Germany and had stopped at Mellanfjärden, one of our favourite harbours, to await better weather. The forecast of a favourable wind from the west or north west prompted us to make directly for Öregrund, avoiding the tricky and inhospitable coast in between. The plan was to sail overnight and enter Öregrunds Grepen at dawn.

Viewed from the north Öregrunds Grepen, the gateway to the Stockholm archipelago, was a great, gaping mouth, formed on one side by the islands of Örskär and Gräsö, and on the other by the mainland. It was about four miles wide at the entrance, narrowing rapidly to a mile off the Engelska light, and becoming a typical archipelago channel by the time Öregrund was reached. The shore along the islands was lit, although there were some offshore dangers. The mainland side of the Grepen was shallow and rock-strewn, marked by unlit buoys.

We saw no problem in an overnight passage. 'Sea Bear' was equipped with Decca and had a much more reliable helming device than that we had installed in 'Bunting'. Joy was fit again and I had as yet no suggestion of the weakness in my shoulders and arms that would trouble us in later years. The wind was expected to reach 10 to 13 metres per second, which would bring it just in to force 6. With an offshore slant that should cause no difficulty.

We reefed in harbour and set off for a fast and enjoyable morning's sail. By early evening the wind had fallen light and although I shook out the reef our speed continued to fall. Now was the time to set Joy's new cruising chute, an oversized foresail designed to work in light winds. Privately I was convinced that the sturdy sailing breeze we had enjoyed had blown itself out and we would have to motor through the night, but I was happy enough to try to keep sailing.

I went on deck to tie down our foresail and our staysail and to wrestle with the cruising chute to ensure that it went up without a twist. Finally it ballooned out and we were off again. I had returned to the cockpit and was leaning back to take pictures of this colourful addition to our sail locker, when I noticed that Joy was taking no interest in this at all. She was looking astern and saying something about a black cloud.

Indeed there was a line of cloud approaching fast and, as it came nearer, it was possible to see a disturbance in the water beneath it. Possibly this was just a squall but it was clear that the cruising chute had to come down again, and quickly. I bundled it through the forehatch, replaced the reef in the mainsail and lashed the other sails down tightly.

When the wind hit us 'Sea Bear' revelled in it, forging ahead at five or six knots under her reefed mainsail. It soon became clear that this was no short-lived squall and that the motor was unlikely to be needed in the night ahead of us. There were two worries: the first that we might arrive in narrow waters earlier than planned and before daylight, the second that the wind would continue to move away from the shore and further into the north, giving us a more awkward and much rougher downwind sail. They were both well justified.

By midnight the seas had become quite steep, causing 'Sea Bear' to lurch about and forcing me to disconnect the automatic helmsman. With a following wind the movement on the boat made a gybe more likely and eventually the boom slammed across with no warning. Joy had been sitting well clear of the mainsheet and the block through which it was led but the force of that gybe drove the block sideways and downwards into her leg. The bone was not broken, but the pain was obviously intense. It was clear that for the time being I would have to manage on my own.

Already the lighthouse of Björn on the mainland side could be identified and the light on Örskär was beginning to show up in the distance. We were about to enter what now appeared more like the jaws of a trap than the welcoming arms of a safe haven. I was all too well aware of those rock-infested shallows on the mainland side.

A possible solution might have been to sail out past Örskär into the Ålands Sea, but the sea outside was itself strewn with hazards. I had only a small scale chart for that area and, worse still, had not devised a navigational plan for that contingency. Now I was in no position for an extended session at the chart table.

There was no alternative but to stay out at sea until dawn was at hand. So I sailed to and fro across the jaws of the Grepen, first to Björn and then to Örskär before resuming our direct, downwind route. Daylight had arrived by the time we passed the Engelska shoals, but it was a grey light that left the passage buoys still hard to see. By 05.30 we could look into the harbour of Öregrund. A gale was blowing straight in between the piers, all was turmoil inside and yachts were attempting to leave. We had no choice but to sail on through the archipelago.

Three hours later we found comparative shelter in Grisslehamn, where we stayed for some days in a wet and muddy harbour, shared with dozens of Swedish sailors whose summer had been blown away by the wind. This rose to a full force 9, and only slowly subsided.

There was no doctor in Grisslehamn, but we found a surgeon on holiday there who was kind enough to take a look at Joy's leg. By then this was one black bruise from thigh to ankle. He bandaged it securely, but reckoned it would be troublesome for at least three weeks to come. The vital question was whether it would be safe for us to go on to Germany, and his anxiously-awaited verdict was: 'Yes, but carefully.' He would accept no fee. Pointing to his own boat moored beneath his house in a wind-lashed creek, he explained that he had nothing else to do just then.

In retrospect there seems little we could have done to avoid the problems we encountered in Öregrunds Grepen, apart from sitting farther away from the mainsheet block. But accidents simply happen and do not always choose the most convenient moments. I certainly misjudged the time of arrival at the mouth of the Grepen. Had we started later it would have been daylight when we got there, but we would then have had to cope with a few more hours at sea in a rising gale. And my failure to have a contingency plan for avoiding the Grepen was related to the time of arrival, since in daylight it would always have been safer to seek shelter in the archipelago, rather than outside.

In the event we probably got ourselves out of that gale and into a safe harbour just about as quickly as we could have done. There was anxiety to be sure, but that was directed more to the extent of Joy's injury than to 'Sea Bear's' ability to handle the situation. And we remained a crew throughout. For all her discomfort Joy managed to find and pass out those sections of the Swedish chart I needed to perform eyeball navigation in the cockpit. Thus she found herself once again staring at the seas heaped up astern of us.

This time they were not great Atlantic rollers but the steep and sudden waves of the Gulf of Bothnia, almost vertical and quite as frightening. Naturally she made no comment: fortunately I was looking the other way.

As the years went by I grew ever less enamoured of sailing against the wind, and positively averse to sailing into the teeth of a real blow. That could be ineffectual and uncomfortable, and often very wet. So it came as something of a surprise, on the occasion of 'Sea Bear's' last gale, to find myself doing just that.

We had by then left the North behind us and were catching up with unfinished business along the coast of France. The ultimate aim that year was to winter in Vannes, on the Morbihan, but on the way we had stopped at a port which evoked fond memories, Fécamp. From there it was a comparatively short distance to Le Havre, to be accomplished easily on one tide. The forecast was for weak winds from the south west, but initially there was no wind at all. We left on the afternoon tide and motored down the coast in drizzling rain, complaining that so much of our mileage in those days seemed to be under power rather than sail. It felt wrong to be using our splendid 'Sea Bear' as a motor boat.

By mid-afternoon we had passed Cap d'Antifer, the approximate half-way mark, and had set a course to intercept the main shipping channel into Le Havre. A suggestion of wind encouraged us to attempt to sail. Yet more might be anticipated since black clouds were gathering in the south. Nothing unpleasant had been forecast for this or adjacent sea areas, but I did not altogether like the look of those clouds.

Although we were already carrying the full mainsail I became more cautious when it came to breaking out the foresail. By then 'Sea Bear' had been fitted with what we thought of as a 'geriatric jib'. This was a large foresail with roller reefing controlled by lines from the cockpit, making it unnecessary to go forward to change jibs, although I had still to go to the mast to reef the mainsail. On this occasion, in deference to those clouds, I left nine rolls in the foresail.

When the wind hit us it was of astonishing strength, rather like the squall outside Skelleftehamn, except that it did not stop: in fact it was three days before it eased to a stiff force 6. It was also blowing from ahead, with a slant towards the not-too-distant shore. 'Sea Bear' heeled alarmingly as I slackened the mainsheet to spill some of the wind and keep her driving to windward. When the squall showed no signs of relenting we had to decide what to do.

The sea was quite flat at the time, but with wind meeting tide it could not be expected to stay so. We could turn and run back to Fécamp, but by the time we arrived the entrance could be difficult if not dangerous. We might stand out to sea and go all the way back to Dieppe. That did not appeal either. Apart from losing all the distance we had gained over the last few days, it would mean arriving in a gale and in the dark. We were however within two hours of Le Havre, and even closer to meeting the entrance channel, from which point we would have a free run into port.

The difficulty was that to sail this course in any comfort we badly needed a reef in the mainsail. And here we were, the two of us with our legs braced against the side of the downwind seat-locker, hanging on with our free hands to whatever parts of the boat offered support, and staring down into the sea on our port side.

If I were to scramble past Joy to go forward to reef, she might well have problems holding the boat steady, so great was the pressure on the helm; quite unexpected in the normally well-balanced 'Sea Bear'. I, on the other hand had by now lost much of the strength in my shoulders. This did not affect helming, but made working above my head very hard and slow. Should there be a problem with the sail, or should the halyard misbehave, it would take time to sort things out, and that could put extreme strain on Joy, while the boat drifted towards the nearby shore.

This was not a scenario I cared to contemplate. It might be the first time I had known that I had to reef and had ignored the call but I stayed firmly put, testing the strength of the wind by playing the mainsheet and sailing 'Sea Bear' to windward as if she were a dinghy.

Within a very short time the calm water turned quite rough, so that green seas came running along the deck and leaping into the cockpit with us. Water that did not flow out immediately through the cockpit drains gathered between the coaming and the locker lid opposite us, so that we were looking into a small lake which could not disperse until 'Sea Bear' righted herself and sailed upright once more.

This she did when we entered the channel into Le Havre and could sail at a more civilised angle, with the wind on our quarter. There she joined a procession of yachts large and small, all heading for the harbour. She romped past most of them of course, because they were very properly reefed. Once inside we got the sail down and found a berth heading into the wind.

And there we stayed for a week while it rained and blew, and we attempted to dry our boat and keep ourselves amused. In spite of all my care one of our mooring ropes chafed through as the wind plucked at 'Sea Bear' and shook her continually. Nevertheless our memories of Le Havre are strangely warm. We watched the *Bénédiction*, the colourful annual blessing of the port, much curtailed in scope and confined to the harbour this year; we found a good baker and a café where we could shed our waterproofs and enjoy strong Belgian beer, even a sailmaker for minor repairs. I suspect that we, along with others, were quite content to be in harbour in that weather.

Later I thought about my failure to reef. In the event it had not mattered. It had, however, been unseamanlike and proof, if proof were needed, of our collective weakness. What could be done about that? In future years it might have been possible for Joy to stay ashore while I sailed with what was described to me as 'beef crew'; possible but unthinkable. We, the two of us, were 'Sea Bear's' crew. She had always looked after us superbly well. If we were no longer capable of looking after her, in any conditions that might arise, we might have to take the hardest decision of our sailing lives. Nothing much was said at the time, but we both knew that we should not wait for the next gale before making up our minds.

CHAPTER NINE

The Game of Looking Back

Forsan et haec olim meminisse iuvabit. Virgil, *Aeneid i, 203*
'One day, may be, it will help to remember even such things as these.'

T ime, when we were sailing, seldom seemed to drag. Our days
were arranged for us by geography and the weather. If we were
lucky we might find a mooring by early evening, which made it
possible to enjoy a leisurely glass of whisky, cook a meal, clear up
and prepare a passage plan for the following morning, before tum-
bling into our sleeping bags.

Even on bad days, when we were confined to harbour by adverse
weather, there was still plenty to do. Provisions had to be obtained
and minor repairs made. The boat had to be kept secure, dry, and as
ready as possible to take advantage of a return to more favourable
conditions. Plans made previously had to be updated with new tidal
information or altered to accommodate a change in wind direction.

So there was little incentive to extend the evening by playing
cards or board games. Unless such activities are enjoyed for their
own sake they can be counter-productive: the very notion of
whiling away time serves to reinforce the feeling that it is hanging
heavy on you. Yet there was one game we played if we had been
kept in port for a day or two, and that was the game of 'looking
back'.

When the log for the day had been written up and any necessary
adjustments made to the passage plan, we would sit in the light of
the paraffin lamp gimballed above the cabin table and read from

the log book the entry for the same day of the previous week, and then of the week before that, and so on. Even on the modest cruises that we made this would show movement, sometimes quite substantial movement. It would prove that we were not rooted to this or any other spot, that we were sitting in a cruising yacht, not a houseboat. It was a short and simple game, and totally positive in its effect.

So now I am thinking of playing it on a larger scale. These accounts of life afloat have so far been arranged in a way that illustrates its varied aspects. These may of course be overlaid one on another, so that the fulmar flits in and out of my thoughts on night sailing, or inscriptions on gravestones remind me of what may lie behind the views of those Finns you meet in the yacht club bar. Yet on the day that it happens the experience has not been assigned to any given category; it manifests itself in a quite random way.

What then if we took a fixed day of the year and looked at what was happening on that date, over a period of some years? That would produce a different perspective on the experience of cruising under sail, allowing it to pass rapidly before us in as unstructured a way as possible. It could not be done for our earlier years, since whatever day was chosen would, as likely as not, find us at home or working rather than on the water. Sailing time was severely limited. But for the eleven years in which we sailed 'Sea Bear' a day in mid-season is bound to see us afloat, in harbour or at sea. Thus I have chosen the thirtieth of June, in the years 1987 to 1998, as our gateway to the past.

Tuesday, 30 June, 1987

'Sea Bear' was new, and our lives afloat were due to start afresh. She had been launched at Itchenor in May. We had spent most of June in Chichester harbour, fitting her out and overcoming the various problems that attend any newly-built yacht. By the end of the month we had left Chichester and were lying at Lymington in anticipation of our first Channel crossing in a Vancouver. The plan was to sail home to Woolverstone along the French coast and across the Thames estuary. Thus for the first time we were contemplating what for sailors based on the south coast was a well-worn routine, a crossing from the Solent to Cherbourg.

The open sea portion of this voyage can take about twelve hours, which means that half of it will be subject to an east-going tidal stream and half to a westerly drift. In an ideal world these would cancel each other out, so that all you would have to do would be to set a course which allowed for leeway, and sail straight there. Naturally it is not so simple. You are unlikely to start at the beginning of one tidal stream and finish neatly at the end of another. And the streams vary in strength at different times of their cycle, and in different parts of the Channel.

It was therefore necessary to draw a passage plan that allowed for these variants on the day chosen for our voyage, but, having done so, I hoped to be able to set a course which we could maintain for most of the way across, allowing the tide to swing us first one way and then the other, and aiming to arrive at our destination by the shortest route possible, which is always achieved by sailing in a straight line.

We were a little late leaving Lymington, but got away by 05.25 on a fine, clear morning with a light westerly wind. We motored out to the Needles to set our automatic helmsman on a course of 190° magnetic, which I had calculated should take us all the way to Cherbourg, provided we maintained a speed of about five knots. This was the first time we had used the more powerful helming device I had fitted to 'Sea Bear', and we were delighted with its performance.

Another new piece of equipment was our Decca set, which had been tested in the Solent. Now it showed us clearly how the strong tidal streams were affecting the real course we were making over the ground. As long as we were being swept no farther than anticipated, which was indeed the case, there was no need to do anything other than to mark our actual position on the chart every hour or so.

For the last twenty miles we had the benefit of a freshening breeze which enabled us to sail close-hauled on our chosen course. So now we had sunshine, wind to sail and a course that should, had the fates been kind, have taken us right into the Grande Rade without touching the helm once past the Needles. Seldom has a new boat had such an auspicious start.

Sadly, I had to take over the helm for the last half mile to avoid being swept right past the eastern entrance. This was the price to be paid for starting late and arriving at the Needles forty minutes after the time I had predicted. But I suspect that if we had sailed triumphantly through the entrance with no hand on the tiller it would have been due as much to chance as to planning. For apart from the near impossibility of estimating the strength of the tidal streams that accurately, how could I have assumed that significant leeway would have been made for only a third of the total distance?

Such thoughts could do little to detract from our general sense of satisfaction at 'Sea Bear's' first Channel crossing. We felt that we had a boat that would do all that we were likely to ask of her.

Thursday, 30 June, 1988

This day saw 'Sea Bear' well on her way to the north. It was not however a happy day, for it was marked by what we came to think of as the 'Tärnö incident'.

We had crossed the North Sea, with pigeons as passengers, explored the Eider River and made our leisurely way to the south of Sweden. Early in July we intended to join an international rally of Vega yachts at Karlskrona, to which we had been invited. In our time sailing first 'Bugle' and later 'Bunting' we had made many friends among our fellow Vega sailors and were looking forward to meeting them again. Naturally our Vancouver could not join in the races, but with that we were well content: our talents did not extend to racing.

Some days had been spent in Simrishamn, with neither of us feeling at all well. By the time we set sail for Tärnö Joy had recovered and was eating again, while I was still battling with sore eyes and a sore throat. In retrospect this may well have soured my attitude to what happened subsequently.

The passage to Tärnö had been pleasant enough but had taken nearly ten hours, so it was already evening when we arrived. We anchored on the spot indicated on the chart, just off a small jetty at which a number of yachts were gathered, and set about preparing our evening meal.

The potatoes were almost cooked when a yacht put out from the jetty and came alongside. The skipper announced that we were in a restricted area and should go immediately to Karlshamn. If I was not sure of the way there through the rocky islands he would guide me and I should follow him.

Had the potatoes not been ready, and had I not been feeling both unwell and hungry, I might have responded more generously. As it was, an argument ensued, the Coast Guard was summoned and 'Sea Bear' was led ignominiously into Karlshamn, to be met by a large policeman and to spend an uncomfortable and noisy night under the walls of a margarine factory.

Even at the time I was surprised at the strength of my reacton to all this. It was, I suppose, a mixture of shock and indignation, with perhaps an underlying feeling of embarrassment at having put myself in an indefensible position. Then however what surfaced was resentment at what I saw as some sort of citizen's arrest and incredulity in the face of a system which banned obvious foreigners from 'restricted' areas, but let in anyone else.

Yet the Swedish yachtsmen concerned were, by their own lights, trying to be helpful, giving up their evening to guide an ignorant Englishman into the harbour where he should have been in the first place. The borderline between helpfulness and officiousness is not always easily discerned, by either donor or recipient.

It took a red squirrel to restore my equilibrium. He appeared from behind the clubhouse of a small yacht harbour on the way to Karlskrona, as if to reassure us that we were welcome in these parts. And the very warm reception we received at the Vega rally in Karlskrona itself served to complete the cure.

Friday, 30 June, 1989

This was a day spent in harbour at Ulvöhamn on the High Coast of Sweden. 'Sea Bear' had wintered in Finland and we had sailed north along the Finnish shore before crossing to Sweden, to witness the sun setting at sea and rising again just as Tacitus had described it. After joining the midsummer celebrations at Mellanfjärden we had set out to explore the High Coast, of which our Swedish friends had spoken with enthusiasm.

We had arrived in Ulvöhamn on the previous day, sailing south from the island of Trysunda against a brisk wind, but in bright sunshine. In the evening we took a stroll through the village with its one narrow street and met the first of our large, silvery hedgehogs. We had found the place quite delightful and were well content to spend a rest day there, especially as the strong southerly wind had yet to ease.

The log book records a day similar to many other 'rest' days, that is to say very busy. I greased the staysail winches, which had given trouble on the hard beat from Trysunda, we did some washing and hung the clothes in the rigging to dry, then we walked into the village to sit in the sunshine drinking coffee and eating delicious home-made cakes. That was when we saw the long-suffering wagtails teaching a young cuckoo to fly.

For exercise, if any more were needed, we climbed the Lotsberget to take pictures of the harbour and walked to the local pizzeria for an evening meal. Now this pizzeria was also a pub, the only one in Ulvöhamn. Pubs of any description were few and far between in the Gulf of Bothnia. To find one in this beautiful place which offered *starköl* or 'strong' beer and the good company of fellow-sailors was an unexpected pleasure. There could be no regrets at being confined to harbour on such a day as this.

Saturday, 30 June, 1990

1990 was the year in which we made our first serious attempt to reach the bottom of the Gulf of Bothnia. I had believed that by wintering on an island in the Stockholm archipelago we ought to be well placed to make the journey there and back in one season. Confident of this I had invited our daughter Katy to meet us in Luleå for a holiday in the far north. What I had failed to take into account was the regrettable habit the wind had of blowing from the north in the springtime, before changing to a southerly direction for the summer.

All went well until we reached Vaasa. Then day after day of strong northerly winds kept us confined to the Vaasa archipelago, until it became doubtful that we would reach Luleå in time to meet Katy on the appointed day. So the plan was changed; she was to travel only as far as Umeå and we would cross the Gulf from Vaasa to meet her there. Her holiday would then become a tour of the High Coast. In spite of our disappointment at failing to reach the bottom of the Gulf, we had no regrets about the prospect of another visit to that intriguing area.

By the end of June we had come south to Järnäshamn, a very small harbour on the mainland shore. Naturally by then the wind had swung round to set firmly from the south. This had given us the chance to enjoy some sparkling, if slightly damp, sailing on the way, but when the wind strengthened still further, it had seemed prudent to stay in Järnäshamn for a couple of days.

There was room here for no more than three or four yachts, so everything was quite informal. Yet the owner of the old pilot house on the quayside had flown a Red Ensign from his flagstaff when we arrived. As far as I can remember this was the only time that happened in the north. Very few people there knew that the Red Ensign and not the Union Jack was the British marine flag. His hospitality went beyond symbolic gestures, and included help with essential shopping and a gift of home-cured salmon.

The friendliness of this place seemed to extend even to the animals who lived among the rocks that surrounded the little stone basin. This was our first meeting with the *skogshare* which, knowing no better and relying on the evidence of our eyes, we initially called a 'rock hare'. The hares would, at times of their own choosing, show themselves to us, much to Katy's delight. We of course were to meet these beautiful and elusive creatures again among the rocks and scrub that bordered the shores of the far north, but never in such numbers as here.

Now, on the last day of June, it was time for us to leave. It was still blowing quite hard, but from the west. We took in a reef and sailed at a brisk pace for Ulvöhamn, since of all the places on the High Coast that was the one Katy could not afford to miss. Eight hours later we were moored in its well-sheltered harbour and ready to show her the 'town'. It was not until the next day, however, that my huge hedgehog – or one very like him – appeared once more, almost exactly a year after I had first met him.

Sunday, 30 June, 1991

Accepting defeat in our first assault on the Gulf of Bothnia, we had retired to the gentle Schlei to winter at Kappeln. From there we had sailed north up the Danish coast, fought our battle with plastic off the Skaw, crossed to Norway and climbed the Telemarks canal up to Lake Bandak, from where snow could still be seen on the mountain tops. Now we had brought 'Sea Bear' back to sea level and were preparing to sail down the west coast of Sweden towards Poland and what had been until very recently East Germany.

The day started at Stavern on the south-east coast of Norway. It did not begin well. We had been there for two nights, avoiding a promised gale. Stavern would have been a pleasant enough place but for one thing; it possessed a disco, situated right on the quayside. Our first night there had meant very little sleep. The noise of the disco continued until 03.00, to be followed by an hour's shouting around the harbour. We survived this only to discover that another disco was scheduled for the following night. Moving 'Sea Bear' as far away as possible did little to attenuate the dreadful din. By the second morning we had had more than enough of Stavern.

Fortunately the wind had eased and the weather appeared much brighter. We left in a light breeze which by mid-day had increased to force 5 or 6 and had become more southerly. A reef was put in and we settled down to a fine sail across the wide mouth of the fjord which leads to Oslo, averaging over six knots and enjoying every minute. A better antidote to disco fatigue could not be imagined.

After some difficulty distinguishing the islands that fringe the Swedish coast from the mainland itself, we found a berth in Strömstad harbour by late afternoon. Then, to our horror, we found that Strömstad too boasted a disco, a large and noisy one looking out over the harbour. Somehow, with a thoroughly good sail behind us, we were a little better prepared to endure yet another sleepless night.

It has to be said that the Scandinavian tendency to site discos in otherwise attractive harbours was worrying to us. It seemed symptomatic of an attitude towards alcohol that might puzzle those living farther to the south. The idea that people might go to a pub for a quiet drink in good company has been slow to take root in Norway and Sweden, where drinking and drunkenness have traditionally been regarded as synonymous. So, where drinking is allowed at all, there seems to have been no limit set to the noise and disturbance it can cause. No doubt to the authorities the harbour is preferable to the town centre for this sort of activity. For the visiting yachtsman it means that some cherished havens have become hell-holes.

Three years later, sailing the High Coast of Sweden for the last time, we heard a rumour that a disco had been proposed for Ulvöhamn. That would be an obscenity. I can only hope that it was no more than a rumour.

Tuesday, 30 June, 1992

We were now ready to make one final effort to reach the bottom of the Gulf of Bothnia. To avoid repeating previous mistakes we had sought and found friends in Luleå who could advise us on where to leave a boat for the winter. Rather than attempt the return trip we were going simply to sail north to the end of the Gulf and to leave 'Sea Bear' there.

From the Schlei we had moved quickly east and then north to Visby on Gotland, from where an overnight passage had taken us to Mariehamn in the Åland Islands. Much of all this had been done under power, so we had been glad of a good wind to let us sail from Mariehamn to Käringsundet, where this day begins. From here we intended to enter the Stockholm archipelago and make for Öregrund, our point of departure for the far north.

Käringsundet was a pleasant harbour. We were already familiar with it because it formed a natural stopping place for yachts moving east or west, rather as Kalmar does, or Öregrund itself, for those voyaging north or south. At such natural crossroads you tend to meet familiar faces and boats you have seen before in the course of your travels. We were however surprised to hear rumours of another British yacht that had been there some days previously. The description given ('old, yellow, with lee boards') seemed to fit one that could normally be seen on a drying mooring off Manningtree. She had left Käringsundet for an unknown destination well before we arrived there.

It was now our turn to leave, motoring west through the chain of rocky islets that extends towards the Stockholm archipelago to leave only a short stretch of open water between Finland and Sweden. For the Åland Islands, although Swedish–speaking and with their own flag, are legally part of Finland; a point brought home to us when we were stopped by a Coast Guard launch and ordered in to the Customs quay on Enskär.

It did not take long to complete formalities there, but the officer who examined our passports remarked that we were the second crew from Manningtree to pass that way in the last day or two. From what he said two things were clear; first, that these were indeed friends of ours and second that in the eyes of Finnish Customs Manningtree must be one of the largest yachting centres in Great Britain.

We left, still smiling at that thought, and hoisted sail to take advantage of a light wind that wafted us across the open sea and into the Stockholm archipelago. There, among the rocks and trees, the wind died away completely. A heavy calm descended and with it a host of flies. At the same time the sky became as black as I have ever seen it in daytime.

The channels that lead to Öregrund are narrow and require careful navigation. I decided that we were in for a thunderstorm and that it would be better to complete our journey under power. Both foresails had been bagged and the mainsail lowered by the time the rain hit us. It was a blinding downpour, accompanied by gusts so strong that the boat heeled over without a stitch of sail on her. We groped our way into Öregrund just in time to find a berth in the crowded harbour.

And there we stayed for some days, until the rain stopped and the wind came round to the south once more. Thus it was that we met Gustav, the owner of a fine, wooden motor boat who had last been seen by us in the Vaasa archipelago two years previously. He presented us with a splendid salmon he had prepared himself, using the warm smoked method which leaves the flesh pink and tender. It was enough for two magnificent meals.

Our enforced stay also meant that we were in Öregrund for the annual Fiskarfesten or 'herring day', when races are held in traditional open boats and the quayside is thronged with people buying fish or knicknacks of various kinds from the stalls set up there. It is a great occasion and one that can be attended only if you have secured a place in the harbour early enough, as, purely by chance, we had. Then, as soon as the wind allowed, we set out on the long voyage north.

Wednesday, 30 June, 1993

Two winters were spent in the far north, so that we could take an entire summer exploring the northern archipelago and the coasts of both countries which cradle it, Sweden and Finland. The end of

June saw us in Kohamn, a nature-harbour on an island at a latitude of 65° 46´ N. The basin there was set in a crescent of densely packed conifer trees. From the shore on one side projected a small jetty to which visiting yachts could moor.

We had arrived the previous evening and had attempted to moor in the customary Swedish fashion, dropping an anchor over the stern and nosing in to the jetty. However our anchor had not held, so we abandoned the attempt and made fast alongside. There was after all plenty of room since the place was hardly full.

What had happened to our anchor reflects much of what might be called the industrial history of the north: it had caught on a log. This was not the first time we had dredged up logs. Logging had been, and indeed still was, a major industry in this part of the world. Farther to the south we had found the quay at Norrbyskär to be spongy underfoot. It was composed almost entirely of logs and compacted sawdust.

More dangerous than sunken logs were those still floating. We had met a number of these on our earlier passage from Vaasa to Umeå. It was not uncommon to meet a tug towing a long raft of logs, with a man in a small motor boat riding herd to nudge the tow round promontories and corners between the islands. In such circumstances it is not surprising that some logs escape, to float for a time just below the surface, and frighten the crews of small yachts.

With all this evidence of logging activity we might have expected to find some areas denuded of trees, but this was not the case. The timber industry works discreetly and young conifers quickly replace those that have been cut down. The trees at Kohamn were particularly dense and, I discovered, uncommonly well defended.

The pilot book indicated that amongst them would be found an earth-closet put there for the benefit of visitors. Once moored I dutifully went to find this in the woods which bordered the shore, only to be driven back by hundreds of mosquitoes. A cloud of them followed me all the way along the jetty where I stood for ten minutes slapping at them until it seemed safe to re-enter the boat and hide behind our netting screens. It has never ceased to amaze me that there should be so many of these creatures in places where there are so few people, but it might account for the enthusiasm with which they fasten on to a victim when one appears.

So we were not entirely sorry to leave Kohamn in the morning, heading for Luleå. Light winds took us to Klubbviken at the entrance of the main shipping channel to the port. The contrast with the place we had just left was dramatic, for Kohamn, in spite of its logs and mosquitoes, had been quite beautiful. Klubbviken itself lacked all charm, while the sight of iron ore ships chugging past on their way to Luleå was hardly inspiring: it would be hard to find vessels more ugly than these.

Of course we were in the wrong place. Just across the narrow channel was Likskäret, the headquarters of the Luleå sailing club. During our stay we were made welcome there and found the clubhouse almost too hospitable. There is a hazy memory of one evening there when Joy got involved in the kitchen, helping to prepare a meal for special guests while I served behind the bar. Anyone who is still encumbered with notions of Swedish solemnity should go to Likskäret to be cured.

Thursday, 30 June, 1994

The log entry for this day is short. We had left the north behind us, traveling overnight from Mellanfjärden, and were once again in Käringsundet. It had been a frustrating trip, motoring into a light, southerly wind which had freshened at dawn to produce a lumpy sea. At one stage I had forgotten to close the seacocks in the heads after use and the log records that I had 'paid the usual price'. Now we had declared a rest day. There was no longer any need to hurry, since we were within easy reach of the Stockholm archipelago where we were due to join another Vega rally before returning to Germany and our base on the Schlei.

It was a fine, sunny morning which became uncomfortably hot as we walked to the village of Storby for some essential shopping.

It is sometimes hard to appreciate just how hot it can get in places where the winter starts so early and lasts so long and where the sea is accustomed to freeze. At the height of summer the land heats up quickly and even the water becomes warm, at least where it laps the sun-baked rocks. It comes as a shock to find that your cans of beer, carefully stowed below the water line, are no longer cold.

Our reward for enduring a sweltering day in harbour came quickly. The wind at last swung into the north, so the next morning we set out for Mariehamn with a good breeze behind us that grew stronger as we ran before it. At one point we found a number of floating nets spread out across the channel. They were suspended from a line of small floats and were so spaced that should you avoid one of them you would immediately find another in front of you. At slow speeds these could be a menace, but we knew 'Sea Bear's' capability and pointed her straight at them.

At full speed she leaped over each in turn quite cheerfully, her keel configuration allowing her to ride the floating line down and let it pass safely astern. There are yachts with fin keels or exposed rudders in which such tactics would have been far from wise, so they are not recommended, however much fun they gave us at the time.

Friday, 30 June, 1995

'Sea Bear' had returned to the Schlei and much work had been done to keep her in good trim. She now had new sails, including our first 'geriatric jib', and a new propeller, so that performance under either sail or power had been enhanced. This year the intention was to see more of Denmark, which we felt had been unduly neglected in the past.

The last day of June found us in the Limfjord. This is the complex series of shallow lagoons stretching across Jutland to link the Skaggerak with the North Sea. It is crossed by road and rail bridges which may open only at fixed times, but offers good sailing. On this day however all it offered was a strong westerly wind right in our teeth, which is why we had decided to stay in harbour in Gjøl.

The log has little to say. Gjøl was a dismal place and its harbour was full of the floating weed that disfigures too many small Danish ports where the water is shallow. It made me think that perhaps I had been right to neglect Denmark so far. However such thoughts were blown away on the following morning, at least for the time being. The wind had shifted towards the north to give us a fine, fast sail, well-reefed, to Glyngøre.

Nevertheless it does seem that Denmark failed to make the impression on us that Sweden, Finland and Germany had done. I have since wondered why this was so. It cannot have been the flatness of the land itself: we came from East Anglia and were used to swapping land for a greater ration of sky. It was not the growing number of wind farms, which formed hideous but still only occasional blots on the landscape. The Danish towns, with their clean and brightly-painted houses were probably the most attractive we found in all our travels. And the Danish sailors we met in faraway places were both kindly and enthusiastic.

I suspect there were two reasons for our relative disappointment. In the first place 'Sea Bear' never wintered in Denmark. Leaving your boat in any country automatically brings you into far closer contact with more people than are met when simply passing through. Then there is what I think of as the 'tourist factor'.

This was exacerbated by the presence of thousands of German yachts in harbours along the Baltic shore. When the time came for their summer cruises they could not, at least in our earlier years, move east. To travel west involved going through the Nord-Ostsee canal and out into the tidal waters of the North Sea, which was not to everyone's taste. So the vast majority went north, into Denmark. This in turn meant that the Danes had little choice but to treat them, and us along with them, as tourists.

Had this not been the case things might have been very different. I recall a visit we made in 1990 to Hasle on the island of Bornholm, a part of Denmark far out to the east and a little way off the well-trodden tourist path. We arrived on a Sunday at lunchtime and had scarcely made fast when we were whisked into the local sailing club and plied with beer and the fish speciality that everyone was eating on that day. A friendlier and less inhibited place would be hard to imagine.

Sunday, 30 June, 1996

By now we were back in tidal waters. 'Sea Bear' had passed through the Nord-Ostsee canal and had explored the River Elbe up-river from Brunsbüttel before making for the island of Helgoland. From there we intended to see more of the 'Riddle of the Sands' country on our way home to Woolverstone. Our first destination was Hooksiel, now sheltered behind a lock opening into the River Jade.

We had waited a day or two in Helgoland, rafted up with others while the wind blew strongly from the west. Now it had eased somewhat and was forecast to be force 5 or 6. That was quite as much as we wanted, but the distance was not great, about 36 miles, and we would be well-reefed, so we decided to go.

The passage plan I had devised was based on the fact that the ebb tide would flow from east to west across the German Bight while the wind was blowing from almost exactly the opposite direction. The tidal streams in the open sea were not too strong so I had calculated that their effect would be to counteract the leeway we would inevitably make. As a result we should be able to sail more or less directly along a meridian southward. Our course would eventually intersect the channel into the River Jade, enabling us to carry a young flood up to Hooksiel. At Hooksiel we should be sheltered from the wind, which would make entry into the harbour quite easy. It was important to enter the Jade at the right point, avoiding any shallow patches, but, quite apart from our Decca, there were two buoys which might be seen on the way to confirm our position.

If this plan should appear a trifle elaborate in view of the comparatively short distance we would have to travel, I can only say that the German Bight is an area to be taken seriously, especially in strong winds and poor visibility. My mistake was not in the plan itself, but in failing to communicate it to Joy in full detail. In fact I was not sure whether the force of the tide would really balance our leeway, and was intrigued to find out before mentioning this aspect of the plan.

We had to wait until the afternoon to catch the tide but finally set out at 14.30, reefed and prepared for heavy weather. It was raining, visibility was poor and the sea was becoming progressively rougher as we approached the estuaries of the Weser and the Jade. Nevertheless 'Sea Bear' remained remarkably steady, so much so that I was lured into my second mistake of the day. Instead of standing, braced against the motion of the boat, I sat at the chart table as if in harbour, checking our position and reflecting happily on how well the passage plan was working. Then, without warning, I found myself in mid-air, flying across the cabin.

Opposite the chart table was our cooker. Fortunately I had rigged a crash bar in front of it, but slamming into a stout, stainless steel bar is still painful. At the time I did not notice any discomfort, because my head had struck the side of the cabin above the cooker and that had knocked me out for a few seconds.

Unhappily Joy had seen all this from the helm, but of course had not been able to do anything about it. Now she was in charge of a boat galloping along at over six knots towards an unfamiliar but distinctly dangerous shore, with what appeared to be an unconscious skipper, and a gap in her knowledge of the next course to steer and the point at which a change of direction would be necessary.

As it happened her anxiety was unjustified. I shook myself, found no damage beyond a few bruises and resumed duty. Nevertheless I had to accept a fair ration of blame for playing navigational games instead of keeping her fully in the picture. It was a reminder, although none should have been needed, of how quickly circumstances can change at sea.

By the time we entered the Jade, it was blowing hard enough to create those unwelcome streaks of foam that signify force 7, and the seas were becoming steep in spite of the fact that wind and tide were now together. We passed two dredgers in the channel but could see them only from the tops of the waves. Once around the corner with the wind blowing off the land all became much calmer.

We had arrived earlier than expected and had to sound our way carefully over the shallows into Hooksiel. In doing so we passed a much larger yacht at anchor, waiting for the tide to rise sufficiently to enter the harbour. Later we were to meet the couple from aboard her. They had just come from Dover, on the last leg of a cruise around the world.

Over the next few days we were able to observe these world-girdlers meeting relatives and friends who had come to welcome them home, and to talk to them ourselves about their experiences. The scope of their achievement made our own efforts seem very ordinary, yet they never treated us as anything other than equals. And indeed we did have one thing in common. We recognised the feeling of anticlimax that enveloped them. It seemed very likely that, on a much smaller scale, our own thoughts might be similar when we got back to Woolverstone. So you have adventures, and then you return and are home again, and so?

Monday, 30 June, 1997

Fortunately the winter had left little time for us to grieve over the loss of our wonderful North. For much had needed to be done. 'Sea Bear' was out of the water and we, as well as experts from the boat yard, swarmed all over her, painting, varnishing, polishing and replacing anything that showed signs of wear. Then, at the end of May, in a boat at least as good as new, we had set out for France.

By the thirtieth of June we had dried out after the gale encountered off Le Havre and crossed the Baie de la Seine to Cherbourg. There we had met Helen and her husband, Chris. They had by then been married for just over a year and were on their way to a motoring holiday in France. Today we were all going out for a sail.

As chance would have it the wind stayed light, so our promised sail became a very modest circuit, out of one entrance to Cherbourg harbour and back in through the other, the only excitement lying in predicting the manoeuvres of the cross-Channel ferries in our path. But it was undoubtedly a happy day.

We were to stay in Cherbourg until the wind allowed us to set course for St.Helier on Jersey and from there to make our way slowly around Brittany to Vannes.

Tuesday, 30 June, 1998

'Sea Bear' had winterd very happily on the Morbihan, although such work as needed to be done had stretched our French vocabulary to its limit. However French engineers knew exactly what to do to cure the stern-gland troubles that had plagued us on the way to Vannes. 'La presse-étoupe? Pas de problème!'

By now we knew this was to be our last season, but before we sailed 'Sea Bear' to Itchenor to be sold we had planned to go farther south, as far as the Spanish border, if the wind allowed. Perversely it did not, so we had turned north again at Les Sables d'Olonne to get the benefit of a brisk southerly. By the end of June we were in Concarneau, having sailed there the previous day from the Île de Groix, in anticipation of worsening weather.

If it is necessary to spend time anywhere waiting for the weather to improve, Concarneau is a better spot than most. The moorings are under the walls of the old town and the whole place is pleasantly relaxed. Our favourite haunt ashore was to become a bar called, I believe, 'Aux Trois Moutons'. It had glass windows which gave the impression of a three-eyed sheep, no doubt to warn patrons of the effects of drinking too much. It was a pleasant place to sit and watch the harbour, or to talk to the resident parrot, although I never had an answer from him.

We were to be in Concarneau, or in ports nearby, for a couple of weeks waiting for the right combination of tide and wind to take us safely through the Raz de Sein and on to Morgat. Although it was essential to take the Raz seriously, the log shows all too clearly that our progress had become exceedingly slow and cautious, with far too high a proportion of it under power. If any confirmation had been needed of our decision to make this our last season, it is there in the statistics. Yet at times I wonder, if we had enjoyed more favourable winds that year, might we not have had second thoughts?

Wednesday, 30 June, 1999

There is no log entry for this day, no log book in fact, and no boat. 'Sea Bear' had found a new owner and we were adjusting to life ashore. Prior knowledge that such an adjustment would have to be made did nothing to make it any easier. The sense of loss was acute.

It was emphatically not a bereavement: boats are not people. Yet it had some of the characteristics of bereavement. There was a persistent feeling that something was not happening that should be happening, that in winter we should be planning a cruise, that in spring we should be fitting out, or buying charts. There was a reluctance on the part of those still sailing to talk to us about our loss, or even in some cases to talk to us at all.

Perhaps bereavement is the wrong analogy: retirement might be a better word. Now I have not yet retired, but have observed those who have, and have seen how, in an instant, they are cut adrift from activities that previously had engrossed them. I have also seen the futility of any efforts they might make to stay in touch.

Naturally there were compensations. Just as retirement brings an opportunity to do something else, something quite new, so we began to do things that had been neglected for the past forty years. We started to take an interest in the garden. We took holidays, the sort of holidays that are common enough but were a novelty for us, driving around Europe, or flying to more distant places.

There was still some sailing. Friends invited us to sail with them on the river at Manningtree or on the Broads. There we were also able to hire one of the immaculate, gaff-rigged half-deckers of Hunter's Fleet to sail the Norfolk rivers, provided that members of the younger generation were there to haul up the sails or lower the mast to negotiate fixed bridges. In this way we were able to recapture the sheer joy of handling fast and capable craft under sail alone. But the 'road to anywhere' we had chosen as our own was now firmly closed.

All that is left of it is a collection of charts and pilot books that I somehow cannot bring myself to throw away, and memories. But memories have value. In a sense they are our only real possessions. We may live in houses, surrounded by things of one kind or another, but these are all external: memories live inside us. So it is that we are able both to keep them as our own and to bequeath them to others, provided only that they are first transformed into words.

Such a transformation is never easy. So many of the experiences held in our memories did not first occur in verbal form. They were perceived directly as sights or sounds or physical sensations. The sting of salt water in your face as you beat to windward, the sound of water lapping past the hull, the march of rugged headlands emerging one behind the other, the dance of islands as you wend your way through a pine-clad archipelago, the ghostly fulmar flitting in and out of the globe of misty light you have created for him, they are all there, but not in words.

Words can at best give an impression of these realities, rather like the shadows thrown on the wall of Plato's cave. The experience itself is however readily accessible to those who want it badly enough. It waits, just beyond the harbour walls, where sunlight lends a sparkle to every wave, all the way to the horizon.

APPENDIX

The Boats we Sailed

The boats sailed in our earlier years will be of little practical interest to readers. However both Vegas and Vancouvers are still being crewed with great enthusiasm by many people, so some notes on them might be appreciated.

The Vega

This boat was designed in 1966 by Per Brohäll. From the outset she was intended for series production, which was at that time a relatively new concept. In the following twelve years some 3,500 were built by Albin Marin AB. We owned numbers 1698 'Bugle' and 3323 'Bunting', both fitted with the Volvo diesel engine which replaced the original Albin C21 petrol motor.

Moderately priced, the Vega enabled many who were by no means rich to engage in serious yachting. Strict one design rules encouraged racing and allowed older boats to compete against newcomers on even terms. Long cruises have been made in Vegas, although the design was influenced by the requirements of the Swedish market, so that the boat was not originally equipped for long distance sailing. There was, for example, no chart table.

Active class associations promoted races and rallies. The International Friendship Regattas held every two years or so in different countries were everything their title would lead one to expect. We attended four of these, and were always made welcome, even after our lack of interest in racing had been discovered.

We looked after 'Bugle' and 'Bunting' with tender care yet, in a sense, we abused them. The Vega was not designed to be weighed down with heavy gear at either end, but for our cruising needs we carried a substantial anchor and as much chain as possible in the bow, while at the stern a bulky liferaft rested on chocks. This made our boats slower and probably wetter than others. Nevertheless their performance in clawing off a lee shore in a Channel gale or riding high Atlantic rollers was impressive.

One modification made life a good deal easier when cruising in hard weather. This was a mainsail which extended to the top of the mast as usual, but came only two thirds of the way along the boom. Such a narrow blade was highly efficient to windward and did not need to be reefed as early as the standard mainsail. Downwind performance naturally suffered, but we fitted twin forestays, so that two foresails could be worn, one on either side, and we could run downwind with no mainsail at all.

The Vancouver 28

In the late 1960s Robert Harris was asked to design a small ocean going yacht for a couple who wanted to sail from Vancouver in Canada to New Zealand. His response was the Vancouver 27, originally made in Great Britain by Pheon Yachts of Newhaven.

The entire concept, apart from a similar overall length, differed widely from that of the Vega. For example, the Vancouver displaced 4,064 kg, against the Vega's 2,300. The extra weight produced a very different motion at sea, and a plumper, roomier hull provided much more storage space. 'Sea Bear' seemed happy to accept whatever we chose to load into her. Having only three berths also increased the space available, although four berth versions could be made, if required.

Mass production techniques would have been inappropriate for this type of yacht, which was built to order and allowed an owner a variety of options within a basic hull design. In 1986 production was transferred to Northshore Yacht Yards at Itchenor. At about the same time the design was modified to create the Vancouver 28, slightly larger and with more space below. 'Sea Bear' was the seventh Vancouver made by Northshore. Altogether about 200 have been built, of this and the earlier 27, and the Vancouver 28 is still in production.

In keeping with the notion of a long distance cruising yacht the Vancouver was fitted with a large fuel tank (127 litres) to supply an 18hp Yanmar GM 20 diesel engine. That made it possible for us to travel under power across the North Sea or the Baltic with no worries at all, should the wind fail. Fresh water tanks holding 227 litres helped to ensure that a cruise was not dominated by the need to obtain water.

Joy and I lived aboard 'Sea Bear' for up to three months of every year. For that length of time she made a very adequate home. Her performance at sea was impressive. Coming off watch for a couple of hours sleep we found no creaking, groaning or rattling noises to cause unease. All was quiet and solid below, whatever was happening outside. She was no racer, and would not go as close to wind as some, but proved her ability to get to windward when this was necessary, and she was capable of fast passages in more favourable conditions. We were more often surprised by arriving early than discomforted by finishing late.

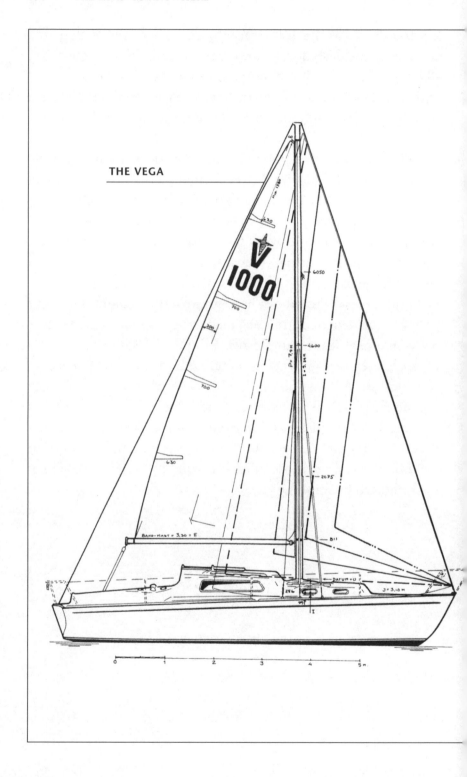

THE VEGA

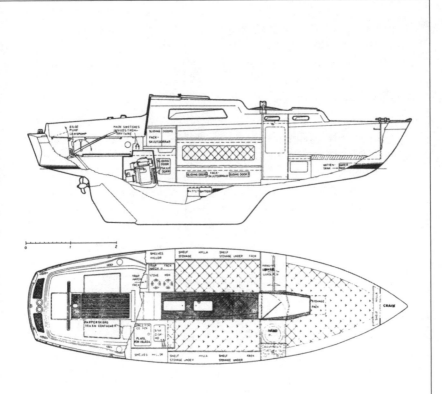

TECHNICAL DATA		
L.O.A	8.25 m	27' 1"
L.W.L.	7.00 m	23'
Beam	2.46 m	8'
Draft, ca	1.17 m	3' 10'
Displacement, ca	2,300 kg	5,070 lbs
Keel weight, ca	915 kg	2,017 lbs
Rated sail area IOR	31.7 m²	341 sq ft
Engine: Volvo Penta 2 cyl. diesel MD 7A	9.6 kW	13 hp

THE VANCOUVER 28

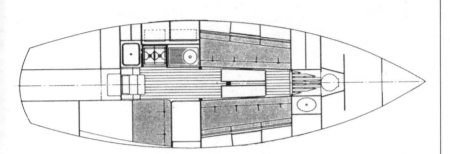

TECHNICAL DATA

MEASUREMENTS

Length overall	8.54 m	28'
Length waterline	6.99 m	22' 11"
Beam	2.63 m	8' 8"
Draught	1.30 m	4' 3"
Displacement	4,064 kg	8,960 lbs

SAIL AREAS

Mainsail	13.6 m²	146 sq ft
No. 1 Jib	11.4 m²	123 sq ft
Staysail	8.1 m²	87 sq ft
Genoa (optional)	28.4 m²	306 sq ft
Storm Jib (optional)	14.1 m²	44 sq ft